PRAISE FOR
Ignite Your Magnificence

"*My perspective has shifted. Reading <u>Ignite Your Magnificence</u> gave me the tools to watch what I am thinking, doing, and saying, and to recognize if I am living in alignment with my true aspirations. If I am not, I now have the way—and wisdom—to get back on track. This knowledge is helping in my relationships, my productivity, and my sleep. Boomers need this book. As I approach year 70, I am finally aware of the value of living according to my vision and beliefs; not those of others. This book provides the tools. Everyone needs this book. If not now, when?*"

-Tom Hailey, Podcast Host and Workshop Leader at The Break Out Session

"*Using a number of metaphors and analogies, Newell gives us tangible examples and easy to apply methods which can enhance the quality of our lives—especially when going through challenging times.*"

-Dina Madi (from Jordan, living in Italy)

"*<u>Ignite Your Magnificence</u> takes Emotional Intelligence to the next level in a most profound way, with actionable tools and real-life examples to discover your Magnificence. Newell takes us on an internal journey to discover our unique magnificence, showing us how to look through our own internal lens as opposed to the lenses of others.*"

-Christine Freeland, Certified Passion Test Facilitator

"Z Newell has a radiant kindness that naturally shines through his story and writing, as he shares tools with the reader that he has used in his life to transform suffering into something beautiful."

-Megan Thompson, CCRP, Sr. Clinical Research Monitor & Yoga Teacher

"*Ignite Your Magnificence* is by all measures beyond magnificent! By sharing his personal journey, the author paves the way for readers to do the same. To own my own MQ means I commit to accepting and loving myself the way I am with all my treasures and flaws. I get to express my MQ in such a way that allows me the freedom to be me and love the Magnificence of others at the same time. Why? Because there's no need to compare ourselves to others. We are each unique and wonderful beings."

-Anita, Passionista, Torres - Certified Executive Leadership Coach & Organizational Learning and Performance Consultant

"Learn it! … Live it! … Love it! … Multiply AHA moments to manifest Magnificence!"

-Cheryl Ann Silich, *American Gladiators* Champion & *Community Link* Radio Host

"*Ignite Your Magnificence* skillfully shows all of us how to become our best self by discovering the harmony our mind and heart can achieve. This well-researched book gives real life examples to illustrate that we all have the power to harmonize our thinking with our heart-centered *passions, leading to a life full of more magnificence. I'll never forget the Magnificence Quotient."*

-Patty Blakesley, Inner Business Coaching

"The principles in the Magnificence Quotient (MQ) are tools I can apply in my life, to be the best version for living a good life!"

-Angela C.

"A sensible, motivating book to help resolve issues that may be interfering with a peaceful, happy and productive life. Well worth the read."

-Ed Walker

"The MQ formula offers us tools to remove the impact of old pain on our present-day decisions and actions. With this heightened consciousness we are able to tap the passion within and realize our true purpose in life."

-Laura Bowers

"With a precise life purpose in mind, Z Newell brings to the table his tried and true methods to finding the Magnificence residing in all of us. Now is the time to honor our feelings as blessings from the Divine and start living our lives the way our Creator intended for us to. Have you had your "aha" moment today?"

-Jennifer Lance

"Through clever and entertaining story, metaphor and analogy, Z lays out a simple but profoundly powerful three component formula that will guide you and keep you on your journey of life discovery, through and beyond the real obstacles. And he does mean your life, not the one someone else said you needed to live, not the one someone else expects you to live, and not the one you were programmed to live based on all of society's notions."

-Randy Crutcher, EdD, Co-author of <u>The Passion Principle: How to Live *Your* Most Passionate Life</u>

Also by Z Newell

BRINK
Don't Go Back to Sleep

Ignite Your Magnificence

the MQformula™
for Discovering Passion,
Purpose and Power IN YOUR LIFE

~ Z Newell

Copyright ©2018 Ivan Z Newell
All rights reserved.
ISBN: 978-0-9962375-3-6 (ebook)
ISBN: 978-0-9962375-2-9 (print)
Publisher: Blue Skyz Unlimited – Lexington, Kentucky USA

Contents

Foreword xi

Introduction 1

1: From Paralysis to Magnificence (My Bout with Botulism) ... 7

2: Our Magnificence Quotient 21

3: Magnificent Moment Under a Magnifying Glass 33

4: Where the Head and Heart Go Astray 41

5: Awareness (The Hive and the Mind) 57

6: The Heart of the Matter 71

7: Life is Beautiful … Until the "Mind Monsters" Come 81

8: Breaking Through to Powerful Action 95

9: More Action Tools for Your Journey 113

10: Mission, Passion and Purpose 121

11: The MQformula — Putting It All Together 127

12: Nail Your Magnificence! 133

About the Author 145

FOREWORD

It is, and it isn't, common knowledge that what's "out there" is not the problem.

So many of us today are constantly buffeted by external circumstance, conditions, and all manner of "problems" that seem out of our control, from quite daunting challenges to just plain minor annoyances. Even those people trying to stay awake and aware are caught off-guard, surprised by the seemingly intractable, unmovable "boulders in the road" that show up unannounced and keep us from living the dream, finding higher ground and purpose—and even having more fun in our lives.

But what's REALLY keeping us back, who's really in control, and whose life is this anyway?

Whether in our own backyard, down the street, in our country or beyond, there surely are situations that desperately need attention, from overheated relationships to our overheated planet. And so, the question becomes, *"Where is our best attention and energy going, and what can we really change for the better?"*

In this book by my friend and colleague Z Newell, you'll find one man's deep dive into an inner terrain where boulders do get moved, buffeting winds are met, then skillfully used to soar higher into a flight pattern that can be charted with more clearly visible and desirable destinations awaiting.

Time and again in this short accessible volume, we are

brought back to one of the most prominent truths about human beings, the concealment or distortion of which I'd hazard to say—in my years as a teacher, counselor, community organizer and world-changer—may be the single greatest impediment to personal and world peace. That truth is that we are each unique, "Magnificent" (in Z's words) and powerful beyond all measure in what we can achieve *on our own terms.*

When that truth is not widely understood, accepted, or in some way withheld from us, we can't do, be or have all that we came here to experience in this one special and precious life. We are constantly battling and in competition for what we think we don't have enough of, aren't enough of. That battle takes its toll on our lives our health, happiness, and ability to make our own unique contribution to the greater good.

Through his own dramatic life, learning as a young man—thank God he survived!—Z was led to an epiphany, an aha moment, that changed his life forever and set the course for the man he would become. He bravely shares that here. Not for the purpose of the all too common, "look at me, ain't I great?" (though he is), but because he cares about his readers (that's you!).

It matters to him that you find the kind of teachers, mentors and inner guidance that help you release old fears and the stories that feed them. Z paves the way for you to apply your own inner alchemy to transform those fears, and to channel your energy into one opportunity after another, so you can learn, grow, love and laugh.

Keep in mind that each of us is inherently good and powerful and, that it's only (big only!) the thousands of daily thoughts in our often under-the-radar personal script and negative self-talk that can sabotage living our best lives.

FOREWORD

Through clever and entertaining story, metaphor and analogy, Z lays out a simple but profoundly powerful three-component formula that will guide you and keep you on your journey of life discovery, through and beyond the real obstacles. And he does mean *your* life, not the one someone else said you needed to live, not the one someone else expects you to live, and not the one you were programmed to live based on all of society's notions.

Z wants for you a life of true Magnificence, yours. He's just that kind of a guy. You can trust this man as your guide.

-Randy Crutcher, EdD, Co-author of <u>The Passion Principle: How to Live *Your* Most Passionate Life</u> and The Divine Dog Wisdom Card Deck and Guidebook

For Otis.
May your Magnificence
ignite the world!

When the Universe was formed,
Two children were born ….
Passion and Purpose.
They were inseparable,
Laughing and playing, loving one another and the world.
They climbed mountains, dived to the bottom of the ocean
And flew through the air as one.
They were Magnificent together, full of joy and inner peace.

Then one day, they began to argue ….
They turned their backs
And began to walk away from one another.
Suddenly, a great quaking began.
The Earth opened, and a giant chasm appeared between them.
Purpose panicked.
His fear grew, his mind began to spin tales
Of how he would never see Passion again.
His doubt consumed him.

Meanwhile, Passion wandered on the other side
Of the great chasm that separated them.
She busied herself for days on end.
She built a hut and went about the business of surviving.
Soon Passion found herself so busy
buried in keeping up with surviving
that she forgot about finding Purpose.

This is the story of how Passion and Purpose
Finally found one another,
How their Magnificence returned.
How together they ignited the world once again ….

~ Z Newell

INTRODUCTION

*"There is no such thing as an enlightened person...
only a person having an enlightened moment."*
-Byron Katie

Right after my twenty-seventh birthday, I became an interesting statistic—one of approximately twenty people per year in the U.S. (that's one in ten million)[1] who fall victim to *Clostridium Botulinum*, more commonly known as botulism—the deadliest toxin on Earth.[2] Once the toxin set in fully, communication between my muscles and nerves was severed and complete paralysis resulted within a matter of hours. I was fortunate enough to survive while my friend, who also absorbed the same toxin, died. (More details in Chapter One.)

My recovery eventually led to a pivotal experience profoundly shifting my view of life, as well as my gratitude for living. From

---

[1] From 1990 to 2000, 160 foodborne botulism events affected 263 people in the United States, an annual incidence of 0.1 per million. No statistics were found for the specific year (1983) that this incident occurred in the author's life. Source: https://wwwnc.cdc.gov/eid/article/10/9/03-0745_article

[2] Botulinum toxin is the most powerful neurotoxin known to date. A single molecule of it is all that's needed to stop one neuron working ... one gram of botulinum toxin would be enough to kill 14,000 people (if ingested), 1.25 million people if inhaled, or a staggering 8.3 million people if injected! Source: http://www.chm.bris.ac.uk/motm/botulism/both.htm.

this single magnificent aha moment the concept of the Magnificence Quotient (MQ) was—unknowingly, at the time—born. Simply put, MQ represents our ability to manifest the Magnificence contained within each of us.

Although my personal exploration began because of a major catastrophic event in my life, this book isn't about facing major challenges. Rather, it's about dealing with those *small* individual moments arising in our everyday lives. By learning to approach those lesser moments in a new way, we'll be prepared when more major struggles show up.

Turning adverse situations, small or large, into healthy growth opportunities isn't always easy. Often, we get distracted by the drama and daily details of our human condition. Yet occasionally we get lucky and have certain lucid moments—known as "aha moments"—a reference now found even in Merriam-Webster's dictionary.

"What was I thinking?" "I never saw it that way before." "It was in front of me all along, but for some reason I was blind to it." These *magnificent moments*, as I refer to them, may be small realizations. However, they can change our perspective and dramatically shift the direction of our entire lives. These experiences range from something as simple as an *"I'll never do that again"* awareness (which we often repeat anyway) to an epiphany or profound spiritual experience impacting our whole life.

It's in our "aha moments" that the world shifts and suddenly gives us clarity.

INTRODUCTION

Ask yourself:
- What if there was a way to increase our receptivity to such moments? To train ourselves to be our own best friend, rather than saboteur?
- Can we capture and experience more of these moments, rather than them escaping us?
- What if there were tools we could use in our daily living to invite in more of these *aha moments?*
- What if there was a clear method to effectively integrate the use of our heads and hearts to arrive at our most empowered state of action in the world?

Try as we might, we can't control all the external circumstances around us; but we certainly *do* have the capacity to change the way we incorporate and respond to the world as it unfolds and confronts us. By mastering the small moments, we can unlock the key to dealing with the more major challenges in life. That's where the MQformula comes into play.

While MQ represents our internal *Magnificence Quotient*, the MQformula is the _process_ by which we manifest our highest potential and MQ.

Instead of becoming overwhelmed or disrupted by events, this three-part process, practiced regularly, creates an internal shift leading to inner peace and, yes, even joy. Utilizing the MQformula process prevents us from stepping into life's pitfalls and losing touch with the vision emanating from our hearts. It's in our hearts that our true passion lays; yet our fears, self-doubt, and limiting beliefs hold us back from living our true heart-sourced vision fully. Using the MQformula we become grounded in the moment and aspire toward our truest vision.

At the core of this very human struggle is the ever-present dilemma between our head and our heart.

- To which do we listen?
- How can we undo the voices in our head that often plague us with negativity, or into believing what we think we want?
- How can we make sense of listening to our heart and deeper passions without guilt or confusion?
- Is it possible to move through—or let go of—our fears, self-doubt, and limiting beliefs?

Which do I listen to ... my Head or my Heart?

The journey of learning to use the MQformula process is an exploration of head and heart. We'll take a much closer look at how these two "tools" function best together to keep us on our path of passion and purpose, and address questions such as:

- *How will I know which to follow and when?*
- *What's keeping me from my own Magnificence?*
- *Where did my fears, self-doubt, and limiting beliefs originate, and how can I break through or let go of them?*
- *Am I using each of these in the most effective way, both individually and in relationship to one another?*

INTRODUCTION

By describing and learning to use these tools fully, we clear the clutter and confusion of our thoughts and emotions. Combining the clarity of self-awareness with the passion deep in our hearts, we'll step into powerful, intentional action in the world. The result is a deeper vision connected to our heart source, from which our Magnificent spirit comes to the surface in our everyday life.

Since the time of my extreme paralysis experience over thirty years ago, I've come to better understand how to face life's adverse circumstances. I've worked through major relationship, financial, career, and personal challenges. *The MQformula is a framework for understanding what happens to us in these situations of challenge*, and about how we can push through our own unique struggles to become more Magnificent.

If you are a seeker of more in life—a person who desires to grasp a richer experience of your time on this earth, or a deeper spiritual experience—the MQformula and its tools is a means to this end. Even if this approach allows you to experience only *one* shift moving your life and a way of being in a better direction, the impact on yourself and those around you can't help but improve the world. And I'll thank you for helping me to move one step closer to accomplishing my mission of creating a vibrant world by inspiring people's Magnificence.

Two important author's notes:

1. *This is not a "self-help" or "self-improvement" book, although you may have found it categorized as such. I don't care for either of those terms; they imply there's something within everyone that needs help or improvement. This subtly leads to*

believing something within us is bad, wrong or not enough. We're all perfect exactly as we are. The problem is that we don't realize this. This journey is one of self-realization or self-actualization of that Magnificence already inside each of us waiting to manifest or be revealed.

2. *The Magnificence Quotient (MQ) and the related MQformula process opens your awareness to receive these magnificent moments as they present themselves. It's a guideline pointing us in the direction of shifting our perceptions and opening our hearts to another way of Being—not to become "enlightened" in some permanent transformative state, but instead providing a running start at raising our level of conscious everyday living.*

So, now we start this journey to uncover the Truth and Magnificence inside you.

CHAPTER 1:

From Paralysis to Magnificence (My Bout with Botulism)

"What lies behind you and what lies in front of you pales in comparison to what lies inside you."
- Ralph Waldo Emerson

One morning, as I sat staring out the kitchen window, looking over my one-acre organic garden in rural Michigan, I had no idea a deadly toxin was creeping through my system. My draft horse was expecting me out in the barn for his daily grain, but for some reason I could *not* muster the energy and I was taking things slowly. Little did I know that my active country life was about to turn into months of lying helplessly in intensive care, depending on a ventilator to keep me alive.

The day before was my 27th birthday and despite the prospect of being too tired for work the next day, I had celebrated heartily with my friends. That morning, my wife Fran had nudged me and asked if I was feeling well enough to go to work. My job at the time was as cook at a local camp. I shook my head and rolled over to go back to sleep. Since we were job-sharing this cook's position, she went in to cover the breakfast meal.

So, there I sat with my coffee, staring out the window. Our three-year old daughter Autumn was still asleep upstairs when I heard a knock at the kitchen door. It was John and Claudia, a married couple I hadn't seen in quite some time, stopping by to drop something off. By coincidence both happened to be registered nurses. Some might say there is no such thing as "coincidence," and they were really "angels in disguise." Whatever the case, looking back, I'm grateful for their timely appearance.

I waved them in as they proceeded to rattle off the typical *"How's it going?"* greeting.

"Wa-bah-da-bu-dah," I replied, a completely incoherent jumble of sounds spilling from my mouth. They looked puzzled, at first probably thinking I was joking. John more closely looked me in the eyes and did a few simple tests, waving his finger back and forth for me to follow and asking some questions. After exchanging a long serious glance with Claudia, she picked up the phone and called a neurologist whom they had worked with at Muskegon General Hospital. A second call was made to the camp to alert Fran, who immediately returned home, and quickly we were on the long thirty-five mile ride to the nearest hospital. My mind was spinning and reeling as I lay helpless in the back of our 1969 Volkswagen camper van.

I don't recall anything about the conversation with the neurologist. My vision was becoming more and more unfocused by the minute, and by that point I couldn't speak except for completely slurred utterances. My world was crashing around me, and I was losing control of the most basic of my senses. The next thing I remember, I was whisked away in a wheelchair and the rest was, literally, a blur. I was so perplexed by the swift series of events that I didn't even feel panic.

I woke up sometime later in intensive care, a ventilator pumping air into my lungs through a tube sticking out of my throat. The doctor had ordered an emergency tracheotomy, knowing that some form of paralysis would soon spread down to my lungs. Being an involuntary muscle, it was inevitable that my lungs would stop working on their own.

I was shocked and disoriented waking up in this strange bed, tubes stuck in me everywhere, and suddenly entirely reliant on my new companion—a ventilator. The machine slowly pumped one breath after another into my lungs. I could hear the rhythmic hissing of its air chamber moving up and down, as it cycled and pushed its life-supporting air into my lungs in a haunting, non-human way. I lay helpless, observing all the medical staff scurrying around, as the paralysis continued to spread. The neurologist was tapping his fingers on my torso, slowly working his way down my body, asking me questions and trying to determine how quickly my muscles were losing their response.

No one was sure of the diagnosis. The neurologist was calling it Guillain-Barré syndrome, a problem with the nervous system that causes muscle weakness, loss of reflexes, and numbness or tingling in the arms, legs, face, and other body parts. The origins of that syndrome are mysterious, but the result is the same no matter what it might be labeled—paralysis. However, the paralysis associated with that syndrome typically moves from the feet upward, while mine seemed to be starting from my head and working its way downward.

They gave me a test for botulism with Tensilon drops to see

if my muscles would respond, but apparently it's somewhat subjective with a wide margin of error. When I didn't react as anticipated, the doctors initially ruled out that diagnosis. Meanwhile, the botulinum toxin was quickly cutting off all the connections between my nerves and muscles. I could still slightly move my hands, so I responded to their questions with a few scrawls on a piece of paper and some questions of my own. *"What's going on? Is this permanent? Am I going to die?"*

Now I felt the panic setting in. I flashed back to my years in college when I'd volunteered for the Red Cross Disaster Action Team. My job had been to attend to the victims of fires, people who didn't need immediate medical attention. I remembered sitting between a mother and child in the back of a police car, the mother screaming, "I just need to know if my other child is dead or alive!"

In that hospital, being in that *place of not knowing* brought more pain and discomfort than everything else combined. I had felt fear of specific things many times in my life, but this dread of the unknown was something I'd never experienced.

Yes, I was perfectly alert and conscious as I witnessed control of my body being swept away. Within a few more hours, all my movement was gone. I was trapped in my own body, unable to communicate, counting the persistent, eerie sound of the breathing apparatus moving up and down, and observing the medical staff scurrying around me with their tasks. The ventilator needed to be constantly monitored and re-adjusted. At moments, I felt like I was gasping for air, while at other times I was swimming in so much oxygen I was dizzy. Each adjustment was tied to another uncomfortable blood test and seemingly endless hours of waiting to get the results and the doctor's permission to modify the machine's settings. All the while I struggled with either the lack, or surplus, of air being pumped into my lungs. Time seemed to slow to a merciless eternity.

The very next day, my friend Mel who lived down the road was admitted to the hospital after having a minor motorcycle accident while on the way to visit me. He was experiencing some of the same symptoms of double vision and slurred speech. The coincidence was too great. The pieces of the puzzle began to fall into place. Word spread quickly to our friends and neighbors back in our town, and that afternoon one of them showed up at the hospital with a fistful of marijuana, trying to save the day. Billy had been growing the marijuana and both Mel and I had smoked it. Billy was convinced that the county officials had been spraying paraquat on his plants and we'd been poisoned. It was a bold theory, and quite brave of him to step forward with this illegal commodity. But we were in some very serious territory, and he cared about us, so he did what he believed was the right thing to help.

Billy *was* eventually found to be responsible for our condition, but it wasn't from the pot. After a lot of further inquiry from the medical staff another important connection was determined. Both Mel and I had been eating some of Billy's homemade soy products. In fact, my wife and I had gone to his house months earlier to assist in preparing and canning this food, which was made from the pulp of the soybeans after processing tofu. The leftover bean pulp was mixed with spices and pressure-canned to create a sausage-like vegetarian food we affectionately referred to as "soysage." Having previously owned an organic restaurant, Fran and I were very conscious about sanitation in food preparation. We were bartering for this food—trading eggs and homemade bread—and we'd wanted to be sure it was prepared correctly.

That one time we'd gone over to help, the jars were sterilized and the pressure-canning procedures followed carefully. With later batches, Billy decided to cut back the processing time by taking a few shortcuts here and there. The monster was created. Three of the fourteen jars in the last batch—as we found out later from the Center for Disease Control—hadn't been processed correctly. The anaerobic (oxygen depleted) environment was the perfect incubator for the botulinum toxin to grow in this high-protein, low-acid food. Yet it only produced its deadly results at the very bottom of those jars. Fortunately, even though my wife and daughter both ate from that same jar, I was the one to polish off that yummy last bite!

Unlike Salmonella (which is what most people associate with food poisoning), there's no gut-wrenching, vile bodily reactions from botulism. Beyond the initial symptoms of discomfort (blurred vision and slurred speech), with botulism there's no physical pain because the nerves are cut off. The real pain is the pain of isolation as all feeling leaves the body, and communication with others ceases. Imagine wanting to talk or ask questions in a fully awake state, but being immobilized in a soundproof bubble. I couldn't even scream. Only my friend and ally, the breathing machine, knew my frustration.

Losing touch with my body and not being able to communicate with those around me—yet simultaneously observing everything going on—was a type of disorientation difficult to describe. It might be likened to the rare occurrence of patients waking up from anesthesia in the middle of surgery. During such instances (referred to as "accidental awareness during general anesthesia") it's been reported that, "Among the symptoms experienced during the event, paralysis was the most distressing to patients—more so than pain". Such occurrences can lead to PTSD from the shock.[3]

The doctors alerted the Center for Disease Control in Atlanta and almost immediately, two representatives were flown up to administer the botulinum anti-toxin. Within a few days the slow process of reversing the paralysis began to kick in. I started to feel my toes and, along with that, a glimmer of hope.

The neurologist assured me I would eventually return to normal. That was comforting until I learned that Mel had died of pneumonia and other complications. He had been angry and afraid, and fought with the nurses and doctors from the minute he was admitted, pulling out his tubes, wasting his valuable energy. Both the medical staff and my family tried to keep his fate from me, knowing it might be devastating. But the nurses seemed to forget that although I couldn't communicate, I could still comprehend. One of them let a comment slip about Mel passing away, and immediately I felt an avalanche of fear cascading over me, burying my growing hope of recovery in darkness.

I pushed past the horror of that news. Slowly, the shock of plummeting from my active country life to complete paralysis, all within a matter of hours, started to fade. As my long recovery

---

[3] http://www.cnn.com/2014/11/28/health/wake-up-during-surgery/index.html

began, I oscillated between panic and hope. I spent two months in intensive care. One morning, Fran showed up to visit and told the nurses that something wasn't right; my neck appeared swollen and she requested the doctor be called. The nurses didn't want to bother him on a Sunday, but Fran insisted. As it turns out, the pressure from the ventilator had popped a hole in my lung, and the entire cavity around it was rapidly filling up with air. They whisked me off to surgery to remedy the situation and to this day, I'm grateful to Fran for saving my life.

But the most terrifying period of all was my battle to be weaned off the breathing apparatus. I even feared falling asleep, so I made the nurses show me the charts of my breathing to convince myself that my lungs were reliable on their own. For very short periods at a time they would unhook me from the machine. My terror slowly began to subside, and hope grew as I entered the final stretch of recovery from my critical state.

After a month I could sit up in bed, and eventually was unplugged for longer durations from the ventilator. Helped into a wheelchair, I recall my amazement at leaving that room. From my bed I could only see a corner of the nurses' station, but now I could observe the whole other, unknown world of the hospital. The plastic end of the tracheotomy apparatus still protruded from my throat as I was wheeled into the waiting room to see my visitors. Although I could breathe through it, I had to cover the tube with a cloth so that the air would pass over my vocal cords in order to speak. Unfortunately I found myself inhaling the cigarette smoke from some of the other visitors and had to quickly be removed.

After seven weeks, I was released to go home for rest and

recuperation. My doctor told me it would be a year before I would have my full strength back and could go about my regular routines. I had lost over thirty-five pounds of muscle lying in bed and weighed a meager 103 pounds, with my ribs and other bones poking through the shell of my once-lean but muscular body. I'd already begun the painfully slow physical therapy process, completely relearning what I'd taken for granted up to that time; walking, raising my arms and other simple movements we make daily without giving it a second thought.

I felt deep gratitude for Fran and all our old friends who regularly traveled from Chicago to help on our farm and support her—while she supported me—through this terrifying experience. The doctors and nurses were, of course, literally life-savers. They performed their duties with diligence, compassion and humor. One day toward the end of my stay, as I lay in bed reading a book on beekeeping, the intercom came on and I heard a loud "Bzzzzzzz," followed by the laughter of the nurses. They were delighted with my surprise and confusion, adding a bit of lightness to my recovery.

My hospital episode was a strangely quiet, yet tumultuous experience—one I wouldn't wish on anyone. In a sense, being trapped in my body was almost a conscripted form of meditation. In my isolation, I had no choice but to observe all that was going on within me. Given that people can generate as many as 60,000 thoughts per day,[4] I became accustomed to

---

[4] In 2005, the National Science Foundation published an article related to research about how many thoughts humans have per day. The average person has about 12,000 to 60,000 thoughts per day. Of those, 95% are exactly the same repetitive thoughts as the day before and about 80% are negative.

observing everything going on around me, but more importantly what was going on *inside* of me. This near-death experience awoke in me a gratitude for life and living to its fullest I hadn't truly and consciously appreciated until that time.

Recovery from this bout with botulism brought me head-on with the realization that *Magnificence* (although I didn't identify it with that word at the time) could be experienced at any moment, and in any number of ways, small or large. My own aha moment came weeks after my return home. The doctor had convinced me that complete recovery would take a full year. This knowledge was like a dark cloud hanging over each passing moment of inactivity. I'd been an active gardener, cultivating about an acre of vegetables, keeping draft horses, milking goats, cutting firewood, making maple syrup, driving the local school bus and, in general, living a very good life.

As I lay in bed one morning watching TV with my young daughter, I thought I would die from going stir-crazy. On top of my already achingly weak body, I could again feel the eternally long recovery time of a year weighing me down even further. I began to tear up, feeling sorry for myself.

Autumn looked at me with her big eyes and said, "What's the matter, Daddy?"

I said, "I can't *do* anything anymore."

To that she replied something to the effect of, "Yes, you can!"

I don't recall her exact words, but Autumn's attitude inspired and shifted me. Suddenly I knew with my whole being that something had to change or I would die, at least psychologically. The next thing, I was shuffling in my pajamas and slippers across the kitchen, and painstakingly putting on my outdoor jacket. I inched my way down the three stairs to the enclosed catch-all back room off the kitchen as Fran ran frantically to the door shouting at me.

"Where are you going? What do you think you're doing?"

"I don't know," I replied, staring at her blankly. "But I have to *do* something!"

I glanced down and saw a hammer lying on a table—no doubt left there by myself months before having come in from the barn after working on something. I wrapped my fingers slowly around it, gripping with all my might as I lifted it from the table. My arm dropped from the weight, but I held onto that hammer for dear life, and pushed my way through the back door and out into the cold, frosty November morning mist. That few hundred feet to the barn was a long journey, passing the huge garden, my old green John Deere tractor, and me shuffling like a ninety-year-old man to the barn door, the weight of that hammer pulling my arm down toward Mother Earth the entire time.

Fortunately, the barn door was open slightly, so I turned sideways and slid in. I could have never budged that heavy door even an inch in my weakened state. As I entered with the light streaming through the cracks in the barn siding, I saw my draft horse, Britemann, leaning over the stall and catching a sniff of his old friend. I hadn't seen him in months after working with him daily. I was grateful for his friendship and company, and I had a feeling that, if he could talk, he would say the same.

As I reached up to pet him, I noticed a nail sticking out of the post where his bridle usually hung. I looked at that nail, then down at the hammer hanging from my hand. *I knew in that moment exactly what I was called to do.* I stepped back and swung my arm up—and failed. After two attempts I used two hands. I swung again and missed. Again. One, two, three, and the hammer glanced off the nail ever so slightly. But I hung on and worked it and worked it, my coordination and aim growing by the minute. *God damn it. I'm gonna drive that nail into this post if it's the last thing I do in this life!*

Swing after swing, I stood there breathing heavily, but with a full and satisfied heart. I had *done something*, and it didn't take a year. In that moment, my whole body knew I had accomplished something. Yes, it was a single nail. But coming from complete paralysis to this point of physically *doing something* was, to me, truly *Magnificent!*

I stood there in the barn, having accomplished one of the greatest achievements of my life by driving a nail into a post. I felt as solid and strong as I imagined that post must feel, rooted in the ground and soaring upward to support the cross beams and the barn roof. In that single moment, I realized that *I must never compare myself to anyone else.* Aha! This was not an Olympic nail-driving competition. It wasn't about driving a nail faster or harder, or better than the next person. And it wasn't about recovering faster than anyone else.

***It was about me, through a simple action,
becoming something greater than I had been before.***

A deep wisdom and profound peace filled my entire being. My "best self" would never be found by comparing myself to anyone else.

I stood there in silence, in awe. My mind flashed on segments of my life intimately strung together. I could see myself as a young child, coming home with straight A's, constantly striving to be in front of the pack. I kept that pace right through college, graduating with the highest attainable summa cum laude honors. On to graduate school I went, where I found myself with a bunch of other twenty-year-old students all *talking* about the meaning of life, rather than *living* it. It was as if each person was trying to prove himself, using his own unique language and framework to protect his wisdom—a tower of Babel leading to more confusion than clarity.

Would I really find the meaning of life through discussion and debate, or would I be better off seeking clarity on my own path?

The pressure and confusion from the competition and comparison had been too much, and I chose to drop out of graduate school. Instead, I turned to a series of life adventures and experiences—something that I could use as tangible material in my search to understand life's meaning, rather than speculate about it. I followed my heart and opened an organic restaurant. However, we eventually fled the craziness of Chicago and moved to this small farm in Michigan so that Fran and I could raise our daughter in a more serene atmosphere.

Now the nail. Deep in the post. As profound as anything I had ever done, and as Magnificent an accomplishment as I had ever achieved.

I must never compare myself to anyone else.

It was from this realization—this simple yet profound aha moment of *nailing my magnificence*—that *I committed to never comparing myself to anyone else again.* And so, the Magnificence Quotient was born. Without consciously realizing it, I launched my quest to bring more *magnificent moments* into the life of myself and others.

Over the past few decades, I learned to see and grasp those moments more and more as they occurred, rather than having them slip through my fingertips. I've listened carefully to others as they described their significant shifting moments, and repeatedly heard comments such as, "It was there all the time, but I just never saw it."

What follows is an explanation of the common denominators forming recognizable patterns leading up to those magnificent aha moments. By following some simple practices, we can increase the chance that life and all its teachings—those often found in our aha moments—won't slip by us. The magic *is* in the air all the time, but we keep ourselves from experiencing it.

We can do something about that.

CHAPTER 2:

Our Magnificence Quotient

"A flower does not think of competing with the flower next to it. It just blooms."
-Zen Shin

In Western civilization, we exist in a culture of comparison from day one of our lives. *"Isn't she the most beautiful baby you have ever seen?"* And the comparisons and competition slowly build. At a certain age in school, we're given an IQ test to see how we stand relative to others in our demographic. This "Intelligence Quotient" is somehow supposed to represent our future ability to be successful. It differentiates us and sets up expectations defining our potential in the eyes of others and, in the end, in our expectations of ourselves.

This obsession with achievement is promoted to an ever-younger audience and is rampant in our society, at least for those privileged enough to have opportunities. These days, with social media as a massively influential tool, the tendency to share and compare has become even stronger.

However, achievement can have its hidden price. I remember while in fourth grade, coming home with a report card that I was very proud of; all A's, except for one A-minus thrown in for humility's sake. My mother's response was, "What happened?" This set the tone for my self-expectation and a standard so high that, although having its positive motivational side, contributed to creating future negative patterns of self-doubt in my own abilities. Although the grading system has its uses for tracking individual progress, it can create the powerful backdrop for comparing ourselves to others at every turn. In some more alternative systems, the students evaluate themselves, with the teacher then giving feedback on the self-evaluation process.

The caution here is to be aware of the additional, potentially harmful self-perception created from comparing yourself to others, rather than just to your own progress.

IQ is Not Enough

Having a high IQ was the pinnacle of achievement and excellence for years until the early 1990s when Daniel Goleman introduced the concept of "EQ" or "Emotional Quotient."[5] The concept of EQ described a new norm for intelligence of a different kind, one in which information and content knowledge plays a much smaller role in personal growth and development than previously recognized. Instead, the framework of EQ recognizes that developing the capacity of understanding the world through our emotional base and relationships can be a more powerful channel for success than pure intellectual-based intelligence.

EQ is largely about *self-awareness*. Briefly, Goleman outlines

---

[5] http://www.danielgoleman.info/topics/emotional-intelligence/

four main components of EQ: (1) Self-awareness, (2) Self-Regulation, (3) Social awareness and (4) Relationship Management. These components provide a skill-set for people to succeed in a way profoundly deeper than mere intellectual achievement.

Like IQ, EQ is *measurable.* We can take a test and compare our level of utilizing EQ skills with similar capacities other people hold. EQ tests, along with a variety of personality test indicators such as the DISC and Myers-Briggs, became more prominent in hiring practices over the past decade. Both IQ and EQ are external measurements that exist *in comparison to others.* A lot of research indicates that a person's IQ remains relatively constant over their lifetime.[6] You're dealt what you've got, so to speak, and that number representing your IQ remains relatively constant through your lifetime. Unlike IQ, however, EQ is a learned skill that can be improved.

Context: IQ to EQ to MQ

MQ has a unique blend of characteristics. On the one hand, like EQ, it can be cultivated and improved. This is great news, since MQ is inherently a measure of our self-worth, and our ability to function confidently and fully in our lives. Yet it's somewhat the antithesis of both IQ and EQ in terms of any standard of measurement. There's no need for charts or graphs to illustrate a person's level of MQ in comparison to others. That is precisely the point; we must never compare ourselves to

---

[6] Research and opinions vary somewhat on this, depending on how IQ is measured.

anyone else, on any kind of a "measurement scale", if we're to truly recognize our own Magnificence and self-worth.

	Measurement	Variable
IQ	External (compares to others)	Remains the same
EQ	External (compares to others)	Can improve
MQ	**INTERNAL (compare to self)**	**CAN IMPROVE**

**To realize your unique Magnificence,
never compare yourself to others.**

Central to this concept of MQ is the critical practice of *never comparing ourselves to others.* To shift our focus *internally* to the source of our own Magnificence, and simplify the sometimes complex and stressful process of living in the world. It's about creating aha moments for yourself and allowing your own Magnificence to reveal itself as you engage more passionately in all aspects of your life.

Working on our emotional skill-sets and becoming aware of our impact on others in the workplace and other social circles, we hone our capacity to self-regulate and increase our effectiveness in relationships. Major companies, such as Google, are incorporating more and more emphasis on developing these skill-sets. Not only do they increase overall productivity by promoting cooperation among employees, the emphasis on these skills increases people's overall level of *happiness*.[7] This cooperative team-building approach and resulting increased engagement and contentment in the workplace helps build people's self-esteem. In plain terms, we feel better about our colleagues, our contribution to the greater good, and better about ourselves.

As individuals, it's perfectly acceptable to strive for excellence in various areas of our life. But we can learn to change *from within,* with the focus on our own improvement, rather than comparing ourselves to others. This shift from perceived values measured by external sources and others' opinions to instead referencing our own internal measure of satisfaction, is critical to developing our Magnificence Quotient.

While it's true that healthy competition can accelerate the development of excellence, constant comparison can erode self-worth. The perspective of viewing ourselves and our progress relative to others—with endless striving, labels of failure, our internal beliefs of not being good enough, and a perspective of lacking in some way—can never properly develop our confidence and self-worth.

The concept of MQ encourages individuals to recognize and experience the *freedom to be yourself.*

---

[7] <u>Search Inside Yourself</u>: The Unexpected Path to Achieving Success, Happiness (and World Peace) by Chade-Meng Tan

We must let go of other people's judgments and standards and focus on our personal path that has brought us to where we stand in life in the present moment. From there, we can then push *through* this moment into a future of becoming something greater than who we were before ... yes, something more *Magnificent!*

At its core, our Magnificence Quotient (MQ) is an internal measurement of our self-worth. Its counterpart, the MQformula, is the *process* by which we increase this capacity so that each of us can shine in our lives.

Viewed in its historical context, the concept of the Magnificence Quotient is a natural evolution which begins with IQ, progresses through EQ, and culminates in the integrated expression of personal MQ. Utilizing the critical tools of self-awareness described in EQ and combining that with a deeper access to our powerful heart-sourced energy, we address and strengthen our internal measure of MQ. Along with that strengthening comes *an increase in our self-worth, self-confidence, and our ability to take powerful action in an intentional way.*

The process of using the MQformula reveals the Magnificence already inside us. The goal of the MQformula is to increase our self-worth and confidence, so that we manifest powerful, intentional action. When fears, self-doubt, and limiting beliefs overcome us and block our potential for Magnificence, our head and heart can't truly work in tandem.

> **It's this *shift in action*—whether displayed overtly in the world or more subtly and internally—that makes all the difference to our sense of self-worth, peace and, yes, even joy!**

To that end, we'll explore in depth the tools of our head and heart, and how they work together effectively to reveal this Magnificence within each of us. However, before we dive into the inner workings and the HOW of the MQformula, it's important to explore two deeper aspects of this topic:

1. WHY uncovering our Magnificence is meaningful.
2. WHAT BLOCKS US from developing this capacity to recognize our own Magnificence and become our most beautiful and radiant selves.

Why Magnificence?

French philosopher Pierre Teilhard de Chardin said, "We are not human beings having a spiritual experience. We are spiritual beings having a human experience."[8]

Whether we attempt a deep philosophical discussion or keep things brief, the simple reality is we often wrestle with the meaning of our existence. We spend our lives on a constant

---

[8] https://en.wikiquote.org/wiki/Pierre_Teilhard_de_Chardin. While there is some debate as to who might have first made this exact statement, several sources as noted in Wikipedia attribute this first to Teilhard de Chardin. It is a commonly quoted saying used by the likes of Wayne Dyer, Deepok Chopra and others.

journey of seeking, consciously or otherwise. We run around looking for the perfect job, relationship, home or environment, the perfect body, or whatever else we choose to focus on. Underneath it all, we share a common search for finding some form of joy or inner peace.

When things go off-track, we attempt to adjust our circumstances and get back on the path of joy, inner peace and fulfillment.[9] *Or sometimes, we may instead choose to stay and suffer.* Often our quest for this eternal state of joy or peace seems so unreachable that we become instead comfortable with the familiar—states of dissatisfaction we gravitate to so easily. When this occurs, we create subtle but powerful justifications within our thinking, and adapt to those beliefs systems keeping us within the limits of what we know.

The stories we tell ourselves depend on the specific challenges we're facing. If it's a healthy body and lifestyle that's unattainable, we tell ourselves it doesn't matter anymore—perhaps because we're married now and don't need to attract others. Maybe we limit our thinking about how much money we can make based on our family's history, or some story that we hear over and over, such as, "You'll never be smart enough to …."

Whatever fears, self-doubt, and limiting beliefs we buy into, they let us accept staying in our comfort zone. And there is always a hidden payoff. Typically, it might require less effort and courage to remain with the familiar. But, along with the seeming

---

[9] Michael Singer's <u>The Untethered Soul</u> is highly recommended reading on this topic

payoff, there is sacrifice. We sacrifice our own Magnificence. We sacrifice the presence that brings out our highest potential.

Facing our struggles and challenges, there's an ever-present tension in our head and heart, of seeking and obtaining, of suffering and happiness. Our attempts to adjust our *external* circumstances can seem both endless and futile. It's only by shifting our *internal* selves that we truly find deep peace and joy. Or, as Eckhart Tolle puts it, "You find peace not by rearranging the circumstances of your life, but by realizing who you are at the deepest level."[10]

To that end, our search for meaning often gets centered in the head or mind. Sure, when everything goes our way, we celebrate by *feeling* good. Our hearts open, we're connected, and our minds relax a bit. However, as soon as our challenges and struggles reoccur, our mind kicks in and our need to understand what's going on takes over. This intellectual pursuit is certainly a part of our human condition. There is also our *heart* to consider—that storage facility for our emotions and cumulative experiences that sometimes guides us without our even realizing it. We may not always know consciously or intellectually what the right answer is, but the option of turning to our hearts for a different type of knowing is always there.

Whether through our head, our heart, or both, this search for meaning in our existence shows up repeatedly, particularly when our pain and discomfort rises to the surface. This is illustrated at its extreme in Victor Frankl's chronicling of his experiences as an

---

[10] Eckhart Tolle, The Power of Now

Auschwitz concentration camp inmate during World War II.[11]

The focus on our "Magnificence" is a framework to put this quest for meaning into perspective. Understanding and practicing the process of the MQformula, we proceed on our unique paths, moving forward with power and intention, and bringing more meaning to our lives. Increasing our effectiveness and Magnificence means making the world a better, more alive and vibrant place for all to share.

What Blocks Us from Our Magnificence

This brings us to the second aspect of this topic; what blocks us from our own Magnificence? The emphasis we place on the importance of our thinking and understanding, versus the deeper wisdom of our hearts, is a large part of this obstruction. Once we recognize there *is* another path to follow (that of the truth in our hearts), the real problem becomes *accessing* this deeper heart wisdom in those moments when our mind so adeptly blocks the way. We obstruct this pathway to our heart with stories we tell ourselves. These stories are so embedded in our belief system that they quietly and subtly control our behavior.

> **The same tools that *free* us to reveal our Magnificence can also *block* us from doing so.**

The word Alethea (Ancient Greek: ἀλήθεια) was used in Ancient Greek philosophy and revived in the twentieth century

---

[11] https://en.wikipedia.org/wiki/Man%27s_Search_for_Meaning

by Martin Heidegger,[12] who some call the father of Existentialism. It's variously translated as "unclosedness," "unconcealedness," "disclosure," or "truth." This book, this journey, is about personal transformation and *uncovering* the Truth of who we *already* are: Magnificent. The manifestation of our personal Magnificence is revealed to ourselves and to others. The question is, "So what keeps us from experiencing our own Magnificence?"

To become Magnificent, we must get out of our own way.

We get in the way of ourselves with our constantly spinning thoughts, and the resulting emotions and stories often throw us off-center. It's those thoughts and emotions, and the belief systems we build around them, that cover up the passion and power living deep in our hearts. Through this book you'll understand how these two beautiful tools—our head and heart—can work together most effectively. The result, our increased Magnificence Quotient (and with that, our very self-worth) gifts us with the ability and confidence to create powerfully conscious, intentional actions. Each of us will step through our doubts, fears, and limiting beliefs, revealing our personal Magnificence … even if only one moment at a time.

We'll look more specifically at how the stories we carry about ourselves in our minds originate and affect us. The power we give to what forms inside our head unconsciously extends and affects

---

[12] https://en.wikipedia.org/wiki/Aletheia

our core belief systems and prevents us from accessing the deeper power buried in our hearts. The process of first becoming fully self-aware of what's happening in our minds, followed by using this awareness to redirect our focus to our hearts, is at the core of the MQformula.

First, however, fast-forward to one moment in time that illustrates the net effect of using the MQformula process. After illustrating such a breakthrough moment, we'll separate it into its significant components and apply those parts to understanding the process described in the MQformula. Once we have the formula's framework to guide us, we'll be well on our way *to walking on our personal pathway to Magnificence.*

CHAPTER 3:

Magnificent Moment Under a Magnifying Glass

"Becoming the observer (step back) you begin to live in process, trusting where our source is taking you. You begin to detach from the outcome. That detachment allows you to stop fighting and allows things to just come to you; you no longer make things happen but allow them to show up. The fight is gone!"
-Wayne W. Dyer, The Shift:
Taking Your Life from Ambition to Meaning

While each of our personal aha moments will differ substantially in content, by definition, these moments are about shifting into a different state of awareness that works in a more *positive* way.

There's a popular saying, "It's all good." People sometimes use this phrase when things don't go quite right, but nothing can be done about that. Essentially, the saying expresses someone's willingness to accept what's happening, even if they don't really like it. A simple translation might be, "Don't worry about it." A person will talk themselves into accepting or moving forward, and tuck that disturbance away—but they never really accept it fully.

Yet, as I recently heard a wise young man say, the real truth more resembles the statement, "It's all good ... *until it's not.*" When the shit finally hits the proverbial fan, that person may not cope with their circumstances.

"It's all good ... until it's NOT."

So, when we suddenly find that things aren't going well, it's too late to just tuck them away. The common response is to let out our frustrations in some manner. We go to the gym and work it off; or we seek out a friend to vent our story. Often, we take it out on someone else, a person who we love because they won't reject us.

However, instead of just pretending everything is okay when it really isn't, *become more aware* of what's really going on and cut right to the underlying, important part of your experience. It's this type of realization that captures the truth of what's happening and more immediately shifts our perception. By doing this, we increase the likelihood of being open to an aha moment.

Here's a story from a friend of mine that captures just such a magnificent aha moment. It clearly illustrates how using these two powerful tools of head and heart together create an increase in our receptivity of such *magnificent moments.* We can increase the quality of our lives through an increase in the frequency and quantity of such significant, enlightened, magnificent moments. [Note: The caution is not to interpret this as controlling our life or destiny, but being *open and aware* enough to receive those moments as they occur.]

Jake's Magnificent Moment

I have a friend who I'll call Jake for anonymity's sake. He's a big, burly guy with a beard, a carpenter by trade.

One day, Jake told me that he came home from work fuming and furious at his girlfriend.

"Did you take the tape measure out of my toolbox and forget to return it?" he barked at her.

"Yes, I was measuring for curtains and I guess I must have left it in the bedroom," she replied meekly.

"Well, I got to the jobsite and couldn't work on the cabinets, because I didn't have my damn tape measure! I lost almost an hour of work driving to buy another one!"

Jake described what happened next. As he stood there feeling his anger rising, his face turning red, he suddenly "saw himself" getting angrier and angrier. "It was as if I was standing there looking down on the whole scene and, in that moment, I heard a tiny little voice ask, *Is this the way you want to treat the woman you love?*

He turned to her and quietly said, "I'm sorry to get so angry. I love you and didn't mean to upset or scare you. Please be sure to return my tools if you need to use them again. I'm working hard for both of us. In fact, I think I'll give you the one I bought today!" He gave her a big hug.

What a magnificent "aha moment." Imagine how that scenario—and their entire relationship—might have spiraled and deteriorated if his anger continued. Instead, Jake changed the course of events for the positive, shifting not just himself internally, but increasing his girlfriend's level of trust, safety and respect for him.

None of those would have occurred without the critical item of his *self-awareness* coming into play. The pivotal point for Jake in his aha moment was triggered by that split second when he saw himself as if he were *"standing there looking down at the whole scene."*

We can learn from this example. Is there a way to break down Jake's experience and take a closer look at the pieces contributing to his shift of awareness and behavior? What is the relationship between this mindful use of self-awareness and the heart's role in creating magnificent moments?

Let's first look at several ways in which our head (mind) and heart tend to interact.

BATTLE. Most commonly, they will *battle* one another. Have you ever felt an internal conflict about a decision that makes perfect sense to you rationally, but your heart simply isn't in it? *"I'll go with this job offer because it pays better, although I really love the way the position at the other company speaks to me."* Or perhaps the other way around … your heart speaks of moving forward, but in your head, you know it's unwise? *"He is such a fun guy to be around, except for those times when he blows up and gets out of control."* This tension is the BATTLE of head and heart. Which do we follow?

BAFFLE. Have you ever felt complete confusion about something that happened? You were hurt emotionally by someone who acted completely out of character, throwing you off-center. Often the battling described above shows itself through our confused emotions referred to as the *baffle* of head and heart. Battling tends to show much higher emotion, manifesting in overt anger or, even worse, anger at yourself. Yet that's often really the result of, or precursor to, the internal confusion we're faced with from our underlying emotions.

BARGAIN. There's another mode of operation, and that's to allow our heads and hearts to *bargain* with one another. Bargaining typically involves some form of compromise such as the heart saying, "I'll eat this ice cream now because I *want* it, and later I'll go to the gym to work it off." In these situations, we attempt to find internal balance through compromise. Our rationalizing process can be simple or complex, but there's always a sacrifice involved.

In each of these instances, be it battle, baffle or bargain, our head and heart are in a tension that's attempting to be resolved. We seek some form of self-justification, or a temporary resolution to get us through our difficult decision.

BELAY: But what if there was another choice? A fourth alternative exists referred to as a "BELAY" of head and heart. Belaying is a method used by rock climbers to safeguard one another against injury. The person climbing and a partner on the ground are attached by a rope and a braking belay device.

One person stands at the base of a rock wall, while the second climbs. At certain intervals she clips into an anchor point on the wall (usually one pre-set by a more experienced climber). This is the safety point to catch the climber if she falls. The rope is fed through this clip and anchor, catching the falling climber, limiting the length of her fall and (hopefully) preventing serious injury.

As the climber continues upwards, there is some slack in the rope. However, the moment she falls, that slack is taken up by the partner on the ground, who might even be pulled momentarily off the ground as he counterbalances the weight. This is belaying—a life-sustaining relationship between the two climbers connected through this rope/lifeline.

It's interesting to note that the climber can ask to rest at any time and let go of her hold completely while her belayer supports her weight suspended on the side of the cliff. In this way, the climber can use the support of her partner to rest and regenerate before attempting to finish her ascent.

Now let's take a magnifying glass and replay Jake's story in slow motion. We'll gain a better understanding of how to prepare ourselves to receive such aha moments in our own lives.

Imagine that Jake's head (mind) is the partner on the ground with one end of the rope, while his heart is the ascending climber. The moment Jake's heart begins to slip and tumble—as his did metaphorically from his rising anger—his mind's *self-awareness* caught his heart. In that split second of self-awareness where he "saw himself," Jake's falling heart was caught safely. It was able to rest and regroup enough to climb back up to the place where the heart is at its best ... replacing anger with love and acceptance from a place of humility and accountability.

Rather than experiencing the *battle* of head and heart, the *baffle* of confusion, or even the *bargain* of striking some form of compromise, Jake's head/mind served him with this magnificent moment of self-awareness and allowed him to *belay* the slack of his falling heart. Although he did fall momentarily into a place of anger and outburst, he managed to recover and avoid what might have otherwise been a terrible outcome.

MAGNIFICENT MOMENT UNDER A MAGNIFYING GLASS

This is the power of *self-awareness*. Practicing and cultivating the use of our mind in this way is an ongoing exercise. Just like any muscle, if we want it to grow stronger, we must exercise it. Waiting until the heat of the moment to use this muscle would be like trying to lift two hundred pounds without notice. However, if we practice this regularly, especially when things are going well for us, it becomes more of a reflex action in more critical, challenging times.

Some people might equate this idea with meditation, and observing what's going on with your mind and body through sitting quietly. Instead, think of this concept as a tool to use throughout our moving, active lives. The purpose behind meditation is to cultivate a mindful awareness to be *used* in the real world, not simply to isolate that practice. Aren't all tools ultimately meant to be *used*, and not sit idly stored away neatly in our toolbox? [13]

Placed in the context of our daily active lives, we use this same practice to *observe ourselves* as we go about our interactions with ourselves and others. In Chapter Five, we'll talk more about this concept, referred to in my first book as the "Watcher." [14]

Practiced and developed at its highest and best, this "muscle" becomes our ally for life. It's the first of two critical tools used to recognize and receive more magnificent aha moments in our lives. The second tool, examined more closely in Chapter Six, is our *heart* and the power of the passion it contains. By utilizing

---

[13] Martin Heidegger's <u>Being and Time</u> is one of the earliest references to the difference between tools being "present-at-hand" and "ready-to-hand," where their actual functionality occurs

[14] Z Newell's <u>BRINK: Don't Go Back to Sleep</u>

the power of self-awareness to clear the path for our heart's powerful energy, we activate a winning combination and turn it into meaningful, intentional and conscious breakthrough action.

Before we look more closely at the proper use of our head and heart, and the relationship between them, here's some pointers on where these two powerful tools can go off-course.

CHAPTER 4:

Where the Head and Heart Go Astray

Where the Mind Goes Astray

This is a hypothetical snapshot of a young child's life. It's an example of how our mind's narratives originate.

Rebecca is the older of two young sisters. She loves her mom and dad, and they love her. They have a typical family life in a suburban neighborhood. Rebecca idolizes her dad and loves being around him. He's very loving and giving, and always does his best to support her. It's a Saturday and he's out mowing the lawn. Rebecca recently turned seven and feels that she's now big enough to do anything.

So she asks, "Can I try, Daddy?"

Being receptive, he walks behind her as she pushes that big mower, helping her guide it until she finally says, "Daddy, I'm big enough to do it by myself."

He lets go of the handlebar and she takes a couple of passes up and down, struggling to turn it at the end of the row. She finally gets the idea of how to maneuver it and heads back toward Dad waiting at the other end of the lawn.

But Rebecca doesn't quite overlap the mower with her previous pass, and there's a small section sticking up between the two clean rows of cut grass. Dad's had a very stressful week at work and must get this lawn finished so he can sit down and focus on an overdue project. Maybe there's even a hidden wish somewhere in Dad's heart that he'd had a son, not just daughters.

Add these circumstances together and Dad snaps at her, "That's enough, Rebecca! You missed in between the rows. Now go back inside."

The impression left on Rebecca is deep. Sure, Daddy let her try the mower, but what remains in her mind is that he dismissed her and pointed out that she missed part of the lawn. He didn't tell her what she was hoping to hear—that she was growing up so fast, how strong she was, and so on. Rebecca is left with the message that she's not quite good enough. Coupled with that, she associates not doing this task correctly with the love for her daddy. The deeper message is that her father doesn't love her (at least in that moment), that she's getting in his way, and she isn't important. Taken to its extreme, not only is Rebecca "not good enough" to mow the lawn, but she's also "not loveable," for one of the most important figures in her world. Still another form of this message is that she's "not worthy" of praise and consideration from her father. These three core messages are some of the most common tapes that people play over and over in their minds as emerging and full-grown adults.[15] These messages lead to a variety of insecurities and self-esteem issues that affect people long-term in their choice of jobs, relationships and other important life circumstances.

---

[15] These core messages are based on my observations participating in forty experiential transformational men's weekends through The Mankind Project over the course of the past fifteen years.

3 core messages people commonly replay in their minds:
- **I'm not good enough**
- **I'm not worthy**
- **I'm not lovable**

Although this is one small instance, the child is very impressionable, particularly regarding her parents or other significant figures in her life. If that pattern repeats enough or is embedded in one larger, perhaps even more traumatic experience, it becomes locked in the child's subconscious and can guide them for many years to come. These pivotal moments are powerful and shape the child's self-esteem and self-worth,[16] building on that cornerstone pattern.

As a young adult, each time Rebecca takes on a challenge and doesn't quite live up to it, she begins to tell herself over and over, *I just can't seem to ever do anything right.* Her self-esteem slowly erodes as she takes on new challenges and her focus constantly stays on "the glass is half-empty" rather than recognizing and praising herself for her efforts and how much progress she's made. The long-term impact might have been completely different if her father said something such as, "Wow, Rebecca, look at you go! I can't believe how strong you are. Good job.

---

[16] For our purposes here, we will consider self-esteem and self-worth to be interchangeable. However, some interesting distinctions can be found at http://www.drchristinahibbert.com/self-esteem-vs-self-worth/ and also http://dalelillak.com/self-esteem-self-worth-and-core-beliefs/. AUTHOR'S NOTE: One way of describing the distinction between self-esteem and self-worth is that self-esteem refers to how the individual feels others are judging and comparing them to others 'from the outside in,' while self-worth is more of an internal measure of one's own value 'from the inside-out'.

Next time be sure to overlap the rows so there's nothing left in between. Now run along and go tell Mommy how you helped Daddy mow the lawn."

This simple exchange with her father came at a time in her development when Rebecca was just beginning to build her self-confidence, yet the core message from her father—as well-intentioned as he may have been—was a negative one. The result is the constant replaying of this story or tape in the background of her mind as she grows up, coloring her picture of herself and her capacity to actualize the magnificent human being she is—particularly when she's facing her life challenges. This core message has the capacity to settle in Rebecca's subconscious mind as well as her heart. At some level, Rebecca's heart was hurt. Her emotional being was damaged, and this energy was stored away in her heart.

In <u>Loving What Is: Four Questions That Can Change Your Life</u>, Byron Katie eloquently states: "A thought is harmless unless we *believe* it. It's not our thoughts, but our attachment to our thoughts, that causes suffering. Attaching to a thought means believing that it's true, without inquiring. A belief is a thought that we've been attaching to, often for years."

What about you? What false beliefs or negative core messages are you carrying around that form stories or patterns showing up repeatedly in your life?

EXERCISE: Origin of Your Story

Take a few minutes to think back to moments that left a significant memory stamp in your mind. In this case, we're not looking for the passionate and powerful memories; rather, seek out those less-remembered moments you'd rather not recall.

Find a piece of paper and write down that vivid memory. Perhaps it was with one or both of your parents, or an older sibling or friend. Maybe it was a bully at school, or even a teacher. Did that experience—or series of repeated smaller ones—leave you with some false or limiting beliefs about yourself?

Now ask yourself some of the following questions:

Who was there? Who wasn't there that you wished might have been?

What did they say?

What part of that memory was the strongest?

Did someone judge you?

Did you have support, or were you left alone?

Were you afraid?

What belief did you form about yourself as a result?

As you reflect on those, don't place too much meaning or judgment on it. Just NOTICE it from a distance.

No blame or shame need be involved here.

Make a few notes of what memories popped into your head before proceeding any further (we will be referring back to this in a later chapter).

_____

_____

_____

How might the beliefs that you formed at that time replay in your life today? What beliefs about yourself are coloring what you think you are capable of now? Do messages such as, "You can't do anything right." "This isn't good enough," "I don't deserve this," or "I'm not loveable" resonate with you? Perhaps your messages sound more like, "No one is here to help me. I have to do everything on my own."

Again, this is a simple exercise, not a life-solving puzzle. The purpose isn't to resolve disturbing or traumatic memories. Just *notice* what thought patterns or messages come up for you. If you're lucky, you've been brought up with more positive messages such as, "You can do anything," "You are loveable and perfect, just as you are." If not, the good news is:

You *can* change the tapes playing in your head.

There are many powerful resources and techniques to further explore the source of your beliefs system. The exercise above, which illustrates core belief formation, is a reflection of the work of Alfred Adler, whose psychology emphasized the importance of feelings of inferiority and the inferiority complex.[17]

Byron Katie's <u>The Work</u> also offers a series of four powerful questions (which we'll visit in a later chapter) designed to shift our perspective on the false beliefs we hold.[18]

I heard the clearest explanation of the origin of our belief system from Michael Singer, author of <u>The Untethered Soul</u>, in one of his talks at The Temple of the Universe.[19]

"We are simply a collection of our thoughts and emotions which we've taken in from our years of experience. Our entire belief system is built on the filters we created for ourselves based on all the stimuli we've absorbed."

Imagine that your head is a computer straight out of the box—not pre-loaded with any software. Now think of your mind as the basic operating system with no additional software or data installed. To understand and interpret the data being input into the computer, such as the sensory data flooding us at every moment of our lives, we must first install software that will make sense of that.

However the only software we install is an accounting system. That will be great for interpreting any numbers, but what will it do if we try to input musical notes? Alternatively, what if our

---

[17] https://en.wikipedia.org/wiki/Alfred_Adler
[18] http://thework.com/
[19] Michael Singer's residence and Meditation Center in Alachua County, FL. https://www.tou.org/

computer is only programmed in black and white, but the data that's entered is in color?

The way that we understand the world (or perhaps *don't* understand it) is based on the filters installed in our basic operating system—in our minds. This is the backdrop of how all our beliefs are formed. If we experience something completely outside of the realm of our previous data and have no meaningful way to process it, this results in confusion—a type of file corruption of our operating system. For example, this is the case for many people trying to process and understand all of the recent changes in our society, such as giving recognition to gay marriages, transgender and other sexual identities.

If something isn't within the realm of our experience, this places a *limit* on our belief system. *We are not consciously aware of what this limit is,* because we have no previous data to process or test it. To do so, we have to install the appropriate software, or possibly even reboot our computer completely!

Our purpose isn't to solve or over-analyze all the problems and challenged beliefs in the world. It's to illustrate that each of us carries a series of beliefs we've formed somewhere along the way. How we *deal* with them is up to us.

The key is to *notice*, on a regular basis, how these beliefs, stories and self-talk show up and affect you.

To move forward with your life and reveal your own Magnificence, it's crucial that you cultivate your self-awareness and catch yourself before false beliefs and stories take over your life.

Where the Heart Gets Lost

Now that we've looked at a snapshot of how these experiences create messages in our minds, we'll go back even further in a child's development to see where these self-eroding patterns begin on an even more basic level—the level of the heart. The heart is amazingly powerful, even more so than we often give it credit for. According to researchers at the HeartMath Institute:[20]

"The heart, like the brain, generates a powerful electromagnetic field ... the largest electromagnetic field in the body," Dr. McCraty explains in *The Energetic Heart*. "The electrical field as measured in an electrocardiogram (ECG) is about sixty times greater in amplitude than the brain waves recorded in an electroencephalogram (EEG). HeartMath studies show this powerful electromagnetic field can be detected and measured several feet away from a person's body and between two individuals in close proximity."

Where does this powerful heart energy go off-track in its development? How does our heart first become buried in the clutter and confusion of our thoughts and emotions?[21] We all begin our lives as newborns with an open heart. We're brought into the world and immediately loved and accepted for who we are. Of course, the world isn't ideal, and many children are born unwanted or in terribly impoverished circumstances. For the sake of this context, we'll assume a welcoming environment and as newborn there's

---

[20] https://www.heartmath.org/articles-of-the-heart/science-of-the-heart/the-energetic-heart-is-unfolding/

[21] Credit for this explanation goes to Geoffrey Atherton, one of the finest mentors I have ever known.

nothing that we can do to be imperfect in the eyes of those around us, because we have arrived—and that is enough.

As the child begins exchanges with those around her, she emanates and receives love and acceptance, typically with no negative feedback.

As time progresses, the infant or young child will inevitably hear a "No" of some sort. Perhaps it's when they start to cry and overwhelm the parent; this varies and may not happen until the child is several years old. But inevitably, some ego-developing boundaries are shaped and the child begins to get some negative feedback.

Heart's protective shield deflects
negative messages to the head

Now think of your heart as a giant storage battery. All the energy we experience from our swirling world of emotions either passes through or is held—either at a conscious or subconscious level—in this battery pack of storage for potential future use. Our heart stores the good, the bad *and* the ugly of our lives. For example, when we've have a traumatic experience, whether it's an incident from childhood or a frightening accident that happened recently, our bodies continue to store that energy and those memories. As many massage therapists know, a person may begin to cry or react emotionally when their muscles and tissues are manipulated. This is because the body stores emotional energy and it often remains trapped until physically released with relaxation or other techniques.

Our hearts serve as the main facility for storing this emotional energy. But constantly reliving the pain or discomfort of the past on a conscious level would leave us, at its extreme, in a depressed and relatively non-functional state. Byron Katie stayed in such a state for years. Her depression and lack of self-worth became so extreme that she didn't even feel worthy of sleeping in her bed. After years of depression and madness, she spent days lying on the floor until, as she describes, a moment when a cockroach crawled across her foot, leading to a major aha moment and awakening[22]

Most of us wouldn't fall to such an extreme. Instead, to survive, we often deal with these painful emotions by hiding, repressing, and denying much of what happens to us. We tuck

---

[22] http://www.dreammanifesto.com/rebirth-madwoman-resurrection-byron-katie.html and/or http://thework.com/en/ab

them away deep inside of our bodies and hearts so that we can protect ourselves and continue functioning.

On some level, we translate our experiences—ranging from ecstasy and joy, to fear and grief—into energy tucked away in this storage facility, this "energetic battery." At any given moment, we have the capacity to tap into this energy. It's relatively effortless to release this energy when your heart aligns with something you absolutely love to do. When a friend asks you, "Do you want to go hiking this weekend?" your passion for nature makes you jump at the chance. If for some reason you have a conflict and can't go, you feel a bit of sadness tugging at you. The positive experiences of those things we love to do are easy to access. We live to recreate those experiences as much as possible, so that we can feel and release that feeling of being alive—that rush of endorphins that comes with doing the things that excite us.

But what about the rest of our experiences? Those uncomfortable, more painful moments have also translated into energy and are tucked away in this storage facility of our bodies and hearts. The expression "broken heart" is one commonly heard, as in the case where we have gone through a romantic break-up or the loss of a loved one. The healthiest response we can have is not to repress those feelings, but to dive into the grief and go *through* the feeling, so that we process it completely, rather than repress it.

A more common response, however, is to store that energy away in our hearts, often turning it into anger and blame, or shutting down emotionally on some level to protect ourselves from feeling the pain. But just because this energy isn't released doesn't mean that it disappears. Rather, it remains dormant and can be triggered by the smallest occurrence.

**In some primary way, our hearts *store*
the energy of our emotions and experiences.**

That energy can be accessed consciously or sometimes triggered unconsciously by our thoughts and resulting emotions (or vice versa), so it makes good sense to look more closely at the *relationship* of our mind and heart and how they can best work together.

Away from Pain & Prose (Story); On to Passion & Purpose

We've examined some of the key ways in which overemphasizing the importance of our mind can sabotage us with messages that don't serve us positively. We've looked at how our hearts translate and store these messages energetically in our emotional center, our heart.

What will we get if we learn to truly access our heart-sourced energy? We claim our PASSION. What will we get if we learn to truly access our mind and use it to align with our heart? We claim our PURPOSE. Aligned and working with one another, our heart and head reveal our passion and purpose.

What keeps us from this PASSION and PURPOSE that reveals our Magnificence?

```
PASSION    AND   PURPOSE
PAS̶S̶ION    AND   PU̶RP̶OSE
PA   I   N   AND   P   R   OSE  (Our "Story")
```

It is the **pain** we hold onto protecting our hearts and hides our true passion. It is the **prose** (or **stories**) we tell ourselves holding us back from our true purpose. Would you rather live with pain and prose, those stories holding you back? Or might your life be better lived with inner peace and joy by revealing your magnificence and living with passion and purpose? Remember, the truth of who you are is already inside you, waiting to be revealed.

Now we're ready to begin assembling the components of the MQformula—to learn how to use our head and heart in a symbiotic manner to create more magnificent breakthrough moments. These moments surround us daily, yet we often don't register them in our consciousness, just as fish take the water around them for granted.

It's important to acknowledge that a large part of developing our Magnificence Quotient (MQ) is the use of our Emotional Quotient (EQ). The EQ component of *self-awareness* is central to the MQformula. That component, combined with the proper alignment and working relationship of our heart and passion, will free us to a new form of action in our lives. One that supports and encourages Magnificence.

Overall, this journey is a developmental progression from IQ, through EQ, to MQ.

Here's a quick summary before continuing. We've looked at the basic concept of our Magnificence Quotient (MQ) and the overall reason for the *process* of the MQformula to manifest our magnificence in any given moment. We've looked at a powerful example of one such moment and broken it down into its major components—the head and heart. Finally, we've taken a slight aside to examine how each of those components, our head and heart, can so easily go astray from their proper relationship and use.

It's time to examine how to cultivate these two critical tools one at a time, first the head and then the heart, so we better understand their interaction and place in contributing to the third and final component of the MQformula—taking powerful, intentional action in the world.

CHAPTER 5:

<u>A</u>wareness (The Hive and the Mind)

"The resting place of the mind is the heart. The only thing the mind hears all day is clanging bells and noise and argument, and all it wants is quietude. The only place the mind will ever find peace is inside the silence of the heart. That's where you need to go."
-*A monk's quote from* <u>Eat, Pray, Love</u> *by Elizabeth Gilbert*

Before diving into our first practical exercise addressing Tool #1, here's an analogy about our thinking. As I mentioned briefly during the story of my hospital stay, I used to keep bees as a hobby. If you've ever driven along a country road and noticed some tall square boxes stacked up, they are probably beehives, or a series of supers (wooden boxes) stacked on top of each other. Contained within the supers are dozens of light wooden frames artificially inserted by a beekeeper. Each frame is started with a single sheet of foundation constructed of bee's wax with a honeycomb-shaped impression that imitates the bees' natural hive structure. The bees then build a three-dimensional comb on this flat foundation base until the combs form a web of honeycomb-shaped chambers. Thousands of worker bees from each hive go out into the world to collect pollen and nectar. The nectar stored in their stomachs is passed from one worker bee to the next until the water content diminishes. At this point, the nectar becomes honey, which worker bees store in the cells of the honeycomb, sealing each mini-chamber comb filled of honey.

The entire purpose is to create enough honey for the members of the colony to get through the colder months for survival, protecting their queen who lays enough eggs to rebuild the colony for the upcoming season. Watching this cycle repeat itself is a bit like stepping back and watching our human activities from a distance as we work to earn money, feed and provide for our families, then repeat this cycle as we support our future generations. On Maslow's scale, this would be the lowest level of physiological survival.[23] Most certainly there is more to the human story than this, but it does bring a smile and perspective to the cycles that we fascinating humans tend to repeat.

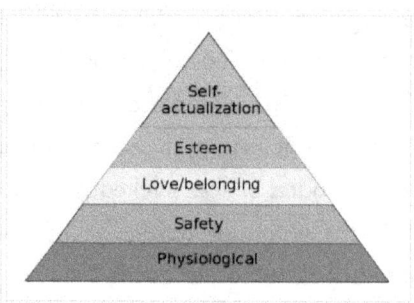

Maslow's hierarchy of needs, represented as a pyramid with the more basic needs at the bottom

Now enter the beekeeper, who helps to create these artificial hives so that she can later harvest the honey, leaving enough for

---

[23] https://en.wikipedia.org/wiki/Maslow%27s_hierarchy_of_needs

the core of the colony to survive and repeat this process the following season. To make his or her way into the hive at any given time, the beekeeper must go through a process to calm the bees down. After all, the beekeeper, although assisting them in setting up this lovely working environment, is still a bit of a predator—their goal is to take away the bees' hard-earned honey!

Before approaching the hive, a typical beekeeper will suit up in all-white clothes, including a helmet with screening to protect their face, gloves, and even white socks pulled up over their pants. Because darker colors represent natural predators (such as bears who love to break into hives), the all-white garb helps to ensure less agitation of the bees. The beekeeper fires up a "smoker," which is a small canister designed to generate smoke from some smoldering fuels. Small bellows allow the beekeeper to "puff" billows of smoke around the bees, which calms them down enough for the beekeeper to open the hive and do whatever is necessary to maintain the hive. Eventually those sealed hexagonal honeycomb cells, full of honey, will be harvested by the beekeeper.

Imagine that your mind is like a beehive, with thousands of thoughts stirring at any given moment, just like those bees! Remember that each of us can have over 60,000 thoughts per day. That breaks down to about one thought each one and a half seconds! The first part of the MQformula process—and the use of Tool #1, our mind—is to develop our self-awareness, which is similar to calming down the bees and observing what is going on inside of us. We are much like the beekeeper in that our task is to actually "step outside" of ourselves and *notice* what is going on. If this sounds like meditation techniques, that's because at its core it is.

However, most people think of meditation as an isolated process; but our lives are much more like the beehive than sitting in a quiet room. Our thoughts, which are often triggered by our emotions (or one might argue, vice versa), are constantly churning up "stuff" that each of us carries from the experiences and beliefs we've developed over the course of our lifetime. We can't escape this. It's as if we started as that completely blank computer and have taken in millions of pieces of data to store away in our minds, buzzing endlessly to the tune of these 60,000 daily thoughts. At any given moment, we may find ourselves and our "thought machines" cranking out dozens of thoughts that can easily become overwhelming. This overwhelm exacerbates our doubts and fears, and contributes to anxiety and confusion, affecting decisions as we move about the world, taking in even *more* new data at every second of our day.

*"When we practice smiling peacefully and calmly,
our peace can permeate the entire universe.
The source of a true smile is an awakened mind."*
–Thich Nhat Hanh

Cultivating our ability to step away and observe ourselves, we develop an ally of sorts … that constant part of ourselves that steps back and observe what's going on within us and influencing our thoughts and behavior. What's critical is that this is a completely neutral observer. *There must be no judgments about yourself as you observe.* If anything, cultivate an inner smile as you notice more and more about your reactions. What thought tangent can you catch yourself going on? Whatever that tangent may be, it's just another one of those 60,000 daily thoughts being generated. What emotions are you noticing, leading you down the path of what mood?

There must be no judgments about yourself as you observe.

The beekeeper is in all-white clothes, remember? The beekeeper must be as neutral and non-invasive as possible. The smoke *calms* the bees; it doesn't agitate them. Picture your beekeeper—your Watcher—observing your buzzing thoughts as you stand back ever so slightly from the hive. Take this one step further. You know that lying below that buzzing activity of your mind is a pot of gold ... the honey that you would love to harvest. The honey lies in your heart, buried below your buzzing thoughts. But first, you must allow those thoughts to either settle or somehow leave your head so that you can access the honey in your heart (more on this in later chapters when we address the heart). Meanwhile, remember that you must allow your "thought storms" to be *observed with compassion*, not with judgment. Otherwise, they will get stirred up even more, creating a fury of participation and further enhancing your involvement and agitation.

The honey lies in your heart buried deep below your buzzing thoughts.

Here's what happened to me one day when I strayed ever so slightly from the beekeeper's traditional methods. Some friends of mine owned a large apple orchard with numerous hives in their midst that had been neglected for some time. The result was that the bees were quite dense in population due to the abundance of fruit trees, pollen and nectar, and the fact that no beekeeper had added extra supers or "rooms" for them to stash all that honey. In addition to these hives being overpopulated, the bees hadn't been bothered for some time by any beekeeper visitors.

Thinking I could handle anything with my super bee-knowledge and equipment, I went over to take a peek ... but I forgot my white socks. I didn't think that would be a big deal. I was wrong. Once I started my smoker and began to stir up the bees, a few of them focused on those dark socks and started to attack. First one, then another, and before you know it, I was literally making a beeline running from the hives with bees biting at my ankles as they chased me down the apple tree lane. I had so many bee stings that I ended up in the hospital with an allergic reaction known as anaphylactic shock.

I'm sharing this with you to illustrate the power of judgment and the harm it can do when cultivating your self-awareness. If you begin to judge yourself for something that you notice, you must *step back* even one more level for your real self-observer to notice that you are starting to judge yourself! If not, that small judgment will alert the other parts of you—just like the first bee discovering how appealing my ankles were to sting—and will begin to pile on more judgments of yourself. Before you know it, you will be running down the lane not knowing what hit you, just as I found myself doing on that bee-filled day.

AWARENESS (THE HIVE AND THE MIND)

Exercise for Tool #1: Meeting Your "Watcher"

*"Every one of us already has the seed of mindfulness.
The practice is to cultivate it."*
-*Thich Nhat Hanh*

The real task is in *compassionately noticing* how the stories we tell ourselves cover up the truth of who we are—a truth lying within our hearts. There are many pathways[24] by which we accomplish this same thing. The exact method we choose doesn't matter, so long as we begin to develop this self-awareness to catch ourselves in the act of slipping away.

Start noticing what's going on within yourself at as many levels as possible. If you're already familiar with meditation, you may have a jump on this awareness exercise. Perhaps you're even thinking that you know all this stuff already, so why not just skip this section? If so, *simply notice that as well.*

If you already have a regular meditation practice, that's awesome. And if you don't, you might want to investigate exploring that possibility. This practice of cultivating our Watcher *isn't* a formal method of meditation. In lieu of formal meditation practices, many people enjoy walking or hiking nature, because it allows them to take their focus off their internal thoughts and replace them with the wonders of all that

---

[24] This practice of mindful meditation is described by Buddhism, Michael Singer's eloquent elaboration of mindfulness in The Untethered Soul, the process of asking Byron Katie's four key questions in "The Work", and also in the practices of the Syd Bank's alternate psychology known as the Three Principles of Mind, Consciousness and Thought.X All of these are powerful recommended practices to cultivate our sense of perspective of ourselves.

surrounds them, helping to bring stillness and quiet to their thinking.

Meditation techniques advocate focusing on our breath or a mantra to still the mind. As our minds wander off, we're encouraged to return to our breath or mantra so that we keep on the path of inner stillness. Yet it's the moment *before* we return to our breath or mantra to focus on here. What part of ourselves is it that catches us wandering off? It's really in the act of *noticing* that our higher sense of awareness is cultivated.

Whether through meditation or whatever method works for you, take a few moments to *notice* what is happening, beginning with your body. Is it tired or aching at all? Is it stiff or relaxed? Go deeper into it. Can you slow down enough to feel your breath … your heart beating?

Go a little deeper. Can you sense what's going on in your stomach? Your gut? Your heart? What do you notice about that core of you that contains that extra "sixth sense" of your intuition? Is there a sense of excitement and anticipation, or possibly a twinge of anxiety or fear?

Now step away from yourself a bit more. Look inside. What emotions are swirling or lying just below the surface? Are you carrying anything with you right now … possibly some feelings left from an interaction with someone recently? Maybe there's an even deeper emotion buried from a past event, such as the loss of a friend or loved one that you continue to carry with you.

Don't judge any of this. It is what it is. Just *notice* whatever you see in your physical body and in your emotional body. Are you anxious? Calm? Tense? Peaceful? Are you feeling anger? Gratitude? Fear? Sadness, Shame? Just notice what's going on.

Watch it. No judgments, only observation.

Now move to the level of your thinking. Become aware of your thoughts. Step back and watch them for a few moments, as if they are clouds drifting by in the sky. What direction are your thoughts taking you in this moment? Are they stuck in the past? Anticipating the future? Are your thoughts moving quickly or slowly? Perhaps you're reading these words right now and deciding you're already well-experienced in this area, and there's nothing new for you here. If so, simply *notice* what's going on as you read this. Or, that you're truly and simply present, relaxed, calm and taking all this in. *Notice that as well.*

Who is doing this watching and noticing? You may say, *"I am."* Yes, that's true. It's a constant level of awareness that remains in the background and has the capacity to independently observe what's going on within you.

This is what we will refer to moving forward as your "Watcher."

It's the same silent observer you've had since you were a child looking in the mirror. This awareness, referred to in ancient practices as "witness consciousness",[25] is itself a constant, yet for some reason most of us are rarely aware it's there because we're caught up in the actual *content* of our thoughts and emotions.

Think of it in this specific example. You are driving along, in a hurry to get somewhere, and you find yourself stuck behind an extremely slow-moving vehicle with no way to pass. You begin

---

[25] https://www.ramdass.org/cultivating-witness/

to get anxious because you're late. Perhaps you even begin to get angry. You start talking to yourself, making up a story about the person in front of you. Maybe you see their gray hair poking up from the driver's seat and imagine an old lady who has nothing important to do in her life.

Now step back and see it from the beekeeper's perspective. Perhaps blow a little smoke into the scene to calm yourself as you begin this process. Begin to *step away from yourself and notice all of what is occurring within you.* Watch and notice your anxiousness, your frustration, how your mind's thought machine is generating a "thought storm" about that old lady. You are the beekeeper observing all of this and you suddenly smile. As you step back and begin to more regularly notice what's happening, *add a smile to your Watcher.* This is a smile of compassion toward yourself—a Watcher who doesn't judge but, if anything, has a sense of humor and compassion about what this awareness is observing.

Add a smile to your Watcher and be *compassionate* toward yourself.

Although I'm suggesting that you "be the beekeeper" and even smile, one caution is not to humanize your Watcher. Don't give that observer a name or a personality. Cultivate your Watcher—which has that capacity to step away from whatever party of emotions and thought storms are occurring within you—so that it can *simply notice and observe what you are experiencing.*

In developing this Watcher, there is one other guideline

besides the importance of not judging yourself. It's critical to *practice* use of it in both positive and negative moments. Remember, even what appears to be "positive" or "negative" is only a layer of belief you're adding onto your raw experience. At times of happiness and joy, take a moment to step away from yourself, as if you were looking down from above, and *see yourself* in that state too. Don't process it, such as having a further conversation with yourself about wishing you were that happy all the time. If that begins to happen, and you have such an internal conversation, step back even further and notice *that* conversation as well.

By cultivating this awareness on a regular basis, this *muscle of awareness* will become more of a reflex that notices what's happening in the heat of the moment—just as Jake did. Keeping this tool present-at-hand[26] becomes more of a natural state for use in those magnificent moments that might otherwise escape you. Think of it as a game, where you are training to "catch yourself" just because you can.

One last caution … this awareness is not about replacing or stopping what you're feeling, or stopping your thoughts. That would be an impossible task! We are human and, by design, in a constant state of movement with our thoughts and emotions. Developing a greater awareness of what's happening within us doesn't mean replacing any of that. *Experiencing* our lives and what's happening around us is exactly the point here. To be joyful in the moment is one of the greatest gifts we're given, as

---

[26] Martin Heidegger's <u>Being and Time</u> is one of the earliest references to the difference between tools being "present-at-hand" and "ready-to-hand," where their actual functionality occurs

the Dalai Lama says. And to *notice* that joy isn't the same as to *feel* it. It's another level of awareness bringing an even greater appreciation to that core feeling. Remember, the overall goal here is to bring more *magnificence* into our lives.

To that end, by beginning to cultivate our Watcher and our practice of self-awareness, we become increasingly free to move in the direction of experiencing the joy and fulfillment contained within those magnificent moments truly in the present. We're seeking to free ourselves from the emotional bondage and psychological thought storms and stories that send us into a tailspin or cause us to miss opportunities. As Eckhart Tolle states so eloquently:[27]

> *"All negativity is caused by an accumulation of psychological time and denial of the present. Unease, anxiety, tension, stress, worry—all forms of fear—are caused by too much future, and not enough presence. Guilt, regret, resentment, grievances, sadness, bitterness, and all forms of non-forgiveness are caused by too much past, and not enough presence."*

Using your Watcher as an ally to observe your internal states encourages this state of being fully present. The primary goal is not just to develop this sense of self-awareness for its own sake, but to *do* something with that awareness. Specifically, the intention is to "belay" our hearts, so that we act fully in

---

[27] Eckhart Tolle's The Power of Now: A Guide to Spiritual Enlightenment

alignment with our passion and visions.

We'll continue this journey by moving on from developing Tool #1, our Watcher or self-awareness, to Tool #2—our Heart. It's through this second component of the MQformula that we access our passions and uncover the truth of what's important to each of us.

CHAPTER 6:

The <u>H</u>eart of the Matter

"Passion is the inner fire that propels us forward... Passion arises from the heart, and your heart's impulse is more likely to be closer to the truth than your mind's analysis."
-*Janet Bray Attwood and Chris Attwood,* The Passion Test: The Effortless Path to Discovering Your Life Purpose

As we begin discussing this next critical component of the MQformula—our heart—remember that the entire reason we focused on the importance of self-awareness as the first critical component was so that we could "belay" our heart. In simpler terms, we are *learning to use our mindful awareness to sweep away the debris and clutter* blocking access to this second crucial component. Accomplishing this, our heart becomes free to serve as the source for clarity of vision, guiding us to breaking through our fears, self-doubt, and limiting beliefs.

At the core of a healthy heart lies passion—a form of energy pulling us towards doing what we love.

EXERCISE FOR TOOL #2 – ACCESSING YOUR PASSION

Picture a time when you felt a passion—perhaps a calling or pull—to do something. Close your eyes and feel where your body resonates with this. Perhaps it's in your heart ... or a tingling in your arms or up your spine. Wherever your body resonates with this excitement, this adrenalin, this feeling of aliveness and passion ... *that feeling in your body* is the tool we're referring to here. Whereas using the Watcher is a tool of looking at yourself from the "outside-in," checking in with your body's natural barometer of your passion is the *second* tool on your journey to Magnificence—an "inside-out" tool, if you will.

When you're *passionate* about something, your body tells you. Whether it's fly-fishing, snowboarding, reading, cooking, helping your neighbor or a friend with a task, teaching someone ... there is a *feeling* that screams out, "Yes! This is what I resonate with. I want more of this!"

To the contrary, sometimes we *know* on an inherent level when we're *not* supposed to be doing something ... something that doesn't resonates with us. This might look like avoidance, anxiety, and fear. Or perhaps it's a just a sense that our job is not the right one for us anymore.

The cues are always there; our bodies don't lie. By consistently tuning into our body, its core feelings and subtle clues, we can utilize this wisdom to our advantage. Anger, sadness, joy, fear and shame should be felt and acknowledged for what they are, along with the physical signs our bodies give us daily.

To review Tool #2, your heart: Tune in to your body, feel

and experience it fully. Listen to its wisdom. Think of this as a way to look at your world and experiences "from the inside-out," where literally tens of trillions of cells are working for *you* on your journey to Magnificence!

Take a few minutes right now to set down this book and just sit quietly. *Feel* all those things that you are truly *passionate* about. Ask yourself:

- What gets my entire body resonating?
- What would I like to do more of, if anything were possible?
- What dreams might my interests lead to if I followed what naturally makes my heart resonate?

Now write down a few descriptive sentences about some of those things with which your heart was just resonating:

_____

_____

_____

If you're interested in a more in-depth experience to further explore your passions, I highly recommend the the "Passion Test"—known as "the number one tool for finding your passions and purpose." There are certified facilitators in a variety of countries who can facilitate this experience.[28]

Sometimes we think about those things we're passionate about as being limited to the recreational activities that counterbalance the stress of our daily lives. For example, you may look forward to hiking in nature as a way to quiet yourself from all of your normal responsibilities at work and home. However, those things or activities that make your heart sing exist in other realms including your Health, Relationships, Career, Spiritual life, Education and Learning, Financial, and Recreation—to name just a few. Don't limit yourself. Dream big. Let your heart speak to you.

The power of the Passion Test experience taught me how to prioritize my own passions.

Some of my personal top passions include:
- Being healthy, vibrant and energetic (because I can't serve others without taking care of myself first)
- Cultivating new and existing relationships
- Travelling and exploring new experiences
- Continuing to learn and grow
- Igniting people's Magnificence!

It took me quite a bit of time to arrive at this short list. I started with very specific things that I love to do, such as hiking and travelling. But as I continued through the Passion Test process, I realized there are more general expressions that cover many of my specific passions. For example, I can "ignite people's Magnificence"

---

[28] <u>The Passion Test: The Effortless Path to Discovering Your Life Purpose</u> by Janet Bray Attwood and Chris Attwood. The author is a Certified Passion Test Facilitator and Passion Test for Business Certified Consultant.

through writing this book, giving workshops, and speaking to groups. I don't have to limit myself to specific activities to recognize there's a passionate energy lying within those individual activities.

No matter what process you use, the main goal here is to *open your heart* to feeling what makes it sing! Your heart is, literally, responsible for your life blood. This is your energy source! It's imperative that you take the time you need, in any way possible, to truly *listen to your heart.* If you haven't done it in the lines provided above, go back and write out some of your passions or, better still, find a Passion Test facilitator locally or online to experience this powerful process.[29]

Perhaps you *are* living those passions you just listed? Or, they're experiences such as "travelling the world" that you haven't any clue as to *how* to achieve them. What's important is to acknowledge what makes your heart beat faster! If you allow your head to block this because of the stories you constantly tell yourself, it's time to change those tapes in your head and allow your heart to be the source of your vision for the future.

A Glimpse of Your Core Values and Purpose

Now that you have named a few specific things to focus on that cause your heart to resonate, take a slightly deeper dive. For each of those things, ask yourself WHY those activities are important to you. What is it about them that's so special to you?

---

[29] Visit https://thepassiontest.com/ or contact the author at z@znewellinspires.com for recommendations

In the examples of my own passions, the underlying ideas those represent for me include such deeper *core values* as:
- Connection
- Love
- Freedom
- Learning
- Leadership
- Fun
- Growth
- Happiness
- Creativity
- Friendship

Now look at an example of reaching the significance behind your passions. Perhaps you love to cook. WHY does this resonate with you so much? Here are some possible associations you might have with cooking:
- It relaxes you
- It reminds you of being in the kitchen with your loving Mom, who also loves to cook
- It's nourishing for you and for others
- People appreciate your efforts when you cook
- Food connects you with those around you
- The power of smell brings back many memories
- Cooking brings out your creativity
- Cooking makes you feel calm and peaceful
- Serving others brings you satisfaction

Some of the *core values* underlying the above list might include:
- Happiness
- Inner peace/harmony
- Connection/relationship
- Pleasure
- Love
- Creativity

On one level—that of the heart—the reasons *why* your heart resonates with doing any given activity aren't important. Truly, it's enough for you to *do* those activities, and not associate them with a reason. Forcing an association just for the sake of understanding isn't necessary. Maybe you love cooking so much that you chose to study at a culinary institute and become a professional chef? Or perhaps it makes you *feel good*, for whatever reason, and that's enough.

The moment we jump from *doing* them, to *thinking* about why we love these activities, we jump from that frequency of our heart up into our heads. In doing that, we risk the danger of over-analyzing and detaching ourselves from the *feeling* we're experiencing. So be cautious about getting caught up in too much analysis.

And yet, it's important for us to make a conscious connection of what lies *underneath* our activities and really drives us, so that we can better prioritize our activities and energy when we arrive at choice points in our lives. Those underlying core values are the "big rocks" that guide us, sometimes more consciously than at other times. Other attributes include Honesty, Integrity, Loyalty, Faith, Respect, etc.—these are some of the deeper guiding forces affecting you. Starting to notice what those are, and how important they are to you, increases an awareness that grows and you'll be consistent in your decision-making.

Since our goal with the MQformula is to better understand the relationship between our heart and our head, with this exercise you'll become more conscious and aware of your underlying motivations and eventually illuminate your purpose. Diving into the underlying *why* identifies the core values of those activities which speak to your heart. Often, there's a common thread and those clues that originate with your passions will point you toward your *purpose.* For example, it might be that in addition to cooking, you're also passionate about teaching. Doesn't that also serve your creativity, bring satisfaction by guiding others, and connect you to them?

Practice noticing and observing what some of your high heart-resonant activities have in common. Maybe you are an outdoors person who enjoys a variety of activities that all share a sense of peace and connection with nature. If this is truly important and speaks to several of your activities, consider applying this same underlying core value to other realms. Perhaps you use nature and these activities to escape from the tension of relationships in your life and work? Instead, actually seek out the same sense of peace and connection *inside* those relationships.

The associations that you begin to make with your underlying *why's* ultimately connect you to the *core values* important in your life. What are you naturally good at that brings you energy and speaks to your heart? Wouldn't it be amazing, if you could tap into this natural energy and passion to power other aspects of your life? Align your underlying core values and purpose more deeply with your work and career? Volume Two of the MQformula series, to be published soon, will address applying this formula specifically to the realm of work and the workplace.[30]

For the moment, become aware that your *what* is tied to your *why* that lies underneath. This underlying reason will eventually reveal your purpose in life, when you follow what speaks to your heart. Cultivate the habit of *noticing* what activities feed your heart, and gravitate toward them as much as possible, so that your heart begins to grow stronger and become a more powerful source for your higher vision in life.

Remember, our goal in this context is to bring your head and heart into alignment with one another—for them to work together instead of creating conflict. Searching for the underlying reasons is a worthwhile activity, but don't allow those reasons to replace the activity of *feeling* the immediate energy and power of your heart.

Keep your heart at the heart of the matter.

We're moving closer to discussing the most powerful section of the MQformula; *taking intentional breakthrough action in your life*. The cycling of information from your head to your heart and vice-versa can be very confusing when they're not in alignment. While we can use our thinking to better understand

---

[30] For a more comprehensive exploration of your deeper purpose, I highly recommend Brandon Peele's recently published Planet on Purpose and his associated online course Ensouled.Life.

the underlying reasons that serve us in a positive way, our mind is also the most powerful source of our confusion. This is where the stories we tell ourselves block access to our heart-sourced vision.

Before we put the head and heart components together into the final "formula," we'll take a little more time to revisit the head component. On the one hand, it clearly can become our ally when we use it to consciously align our purpose with our passions and to cultivate the tool of self-awareness. On the other hand, it also contains a darker side that can plague and trick us into falling away from our heart-sourced vision.

CHAPTER 7:

Life is Beautiful ... Until the "Mind Monsters" Come

"The irony is that we attempt to disown our difficult stories to appear more whole or more acceptable, but our wholeness—even our wholeheartedness—actually depends on the integration of all our experiences, INCLUDING THE FALLS."
- *Brené Brown*

It seems that all we need to do to have an amazingly Magnificent life is to ignite and follow our heart and natural passions, then dig in to understand why these are important. Once we do this, we magically find our purpose and life is beautiful. Our heart-sourced vision and our head's understanding of our purpose are in perfect alignment. Life magically unfolds. Our relationships are fulfilling, our work and career resonate with our heart, and everything is perfect.

While all of this may sound great, the truth is that there are relatively few people for whom the above happens. Yes, for them life may appear to be Magnificent. If you think that those people are lucky, think again. Perhaps they were born into some golden circumstances, but I have no doubt that each of them has their own fears, self-doubt, and limiting beliefs, no matter how successful they appear from the outside looking into their lives.

The MQformula is designed as a framework to understand conceptually how to arrive at that place where life is flowing. A more accurate description would be *how to journey to that place*, since it's an ongoing process, not a destination.

Along this journey we need a strategy to deal with ….

Slaying the 3-Headed Mind Monster

Before we pull together the final components of the MQformula, revisit that very complex and often tricky first component; your head. The very first step in any battle with an enemy is to *become aware* of its presence.

Fears, self-doubt, and limiting beliefs run rampant in our minds. For our discussion here, I'm going to affectionately dub this powerful triad our "Three-Headed Mind Monster." Until you can master catching these mind monsters with your Watcher (our #1 tool of self-awareness), they'll rise up to create the stress and conflict that creates a continuous head-heart dilemma.

What is the nature of these self-tormenting thoughts?

- Fears: those apparently *external* factors that the world throws at us
- Self-doubt: those *internal* self-questioning stories that constantly reoccur
- Limiting beliefs: those *overall* factors that blanket our entire understanding

Remember the quote from Byron Katie at the very beginning of this book:

"There is no such thing as an enlightened person...
only a person having an enlightened moment."

The process of the MQformula is an ongoing one. By using and practicing the steps outlined in the third component of this formula, you'll be able to defeat some of these mind monsters, or at the very least become more aware of how to keep them at bay and let your heart to shine.

We place an enormous amount of significance on what's inside our head. This is the fallacy of the IQ mentioned earlier. The reality is that your head has a "mind of its own" which seems to believe it's smarter than you are. For some reason, it's chosen the task of guarding and protecting your heart. Just as we described with the little girl helping her father mow the lawn, we create stories that we *believe* will serve us. These stories are generated out of a framework that is very, very difficult to break through. They originate from a self-protective place when we're vulnerable, and subconsciously become the stories that serve to guide and presumably protect us.

To better understand what goes on in our heads as we struggle along on this journey, there are two different paths to explore:
- Where did those stories originate?
- How can you best deal with them?

Where Did Your Stories Originate?

Asking the first of these questions is the approach that most traditional therapies and counseling offer. There's nothing wrong with delving into our past to identify some of the core sources of our internal storytelling. Recall one of the earlier exercises in Chapter Four where you delved back into your memories to get a glimpse of where some of your earliest beliefs were formed. (If you didn't participate in that exercise, take a few minutes to go back now and take a closer look.) Maintaining an awareness of this origin is helpful in recognizing the patterns in you.

Earlier, I told the story of coming home with my report card consisting of all A's and one A-minus. For decades I've incorporated my mother's expectation of perfection into my life, creating goals for myself so high that my focus has always been on that last piece of my performance that's not quite good enough. It sometimes seems that, even if the glass were spilling over with good things, I could still find something wrong with that!

Funny, isn't it? Looking from the outside in, someone might observe my circumstances and be envious of how good things are, but my *internal expectations* and those stories spinning in my mind are what dictates my reality (or at least have for decades, which is why I now share some of those solutions with you here). Even in this very moment, as I write this book, a part of me questions what might be wrong, missing or not good enough. However, if I keep the MQ principle of **never comparing myself to another**, I'll maintain my internal balance and sense of self-worth.

How Can You Best Deal With Your Stories?

Now that we have at least a brief reference to the origin of some of those stories running in your head, return to the key question: "How can you best deal with them?" or, "What are you going to *do* about these stories?"

In some respects, the phrase *slaying the mind monsters* isn't accurate. The truth is we'll never destroy them. As Brené Brown's quote at the beginning of this chapter describes, we must *incorporate* them into our world. We must learn to take the falls that come our way in a more gracious and flowing manner.

Look back at what you wrote in the "Origin of Your Story" exercise and ask yourself how you look at those early memories now. Do you experience some form of irritation, or even mild trauma, when you think back on those? Or can you possibly laugh at them more easily now? Are you still holding negative energy toward the people who may have harmed you, abandoned you, or even unknowingly helped to form this image of yourself that you've held onto all this time? Is it time to let go and forgive them? Or more important, to forgive *yourself*?

Believe it or not, of those 60,000+ daily thoughts, approximately ninety percent are recurring ones (or those taking a very similar form of self-criticism.) The real challenge isn't in delving back into the source of negative stories, but rather how to best deal with them when they return.

No matter how hard we try, we can't control the thoughts that pop up in our heads. We *can* reprogram ourselves to some extent, as the neuro-linguistic programming (NLP) approach takes. We can create powerful exercises to rationalize and understand our fears, and create positive affirmations to reinforce our positive mental attitude.

But the mind monsters will invariably rise again.

Studying martial arts is a perfect analogy for finding a practical approach to best deal with these internal stories. Those who study various forms of martial arts know that learning to fall correctly is one of the key ingredients to succeeding. Others might say that the key is getting back up again. Both are true. Here I will share my own experience of studying Aikido, which some refer to as "the peaceful martial art."

Fight, Flight or Freeze… A Fourth Alternative

Imagine that a force of some kind is coming directly at you. Typically, in life, there are three main options that occur:
- Fight
- Flight
- Freeze

The first option—to fight—requires a lot of energy to block and counter the force coming at you. It means facing your fear and countering with a force stronger than your opponent's. To do so either calls for a huge burst of adrenaline or some serious training.

The second option—to flee—is a natural one built into our survival system since primitive man. We know this portion of our brain as the amygdala. "When you think of the amygdala, you should think of one word. *Fear*. The amygdala is the reason we are afraid of things outside our control. It also controls the way we react to certain *stimuli*, or an event that causes an emotion, that we see as potentially threatening or dangerous."[31]

The third option—to freeze—is yet another way that we deal (or don't deal) with our fear. This might look like physically standing still in a dangerous situation, or it might take the subtler form of avoidance or procrastination. Essentially, we make no movement in our life so that we don't endanger ourselves.

But what if there were a fourth option? This is precisely what the art of Aikido demonstrates: *Flow*. Imagine again that force coming at you. This force is a person, and in slow motion they are delivering a punch directly to your stomach. Rather than fight, flee or freeze, picture the following ….

As you see the clenched fist coming directly at you, you shift one foot back, pivoting slightly "off the line" so that the blow instead narrowly grazes you. To keep this illustration clear, imagine that you step your right foot back to about a forty-five degree angle, so that your body is slightly sideways to the punch, instead of directly facing it.

---

[31] http://brainmadesimple.com/amygdala.html

Now take your right arm and extend it so that it parallels the arm of your attacker. As you do this, *you become one with the force itself.* By literally stepping to the side and aligning yourself with the opposing force, you are in a perfect position to turn it against itself.

The final step is to add just enough force to redirect the blow. With a gentle movement requiring very little energy, you grasp your opponent's arm and redirect the force in a circle, then add a slight reversing action to bring them to the ground in an almost effortless, flowing movement.

I have watched Alice, a short, hundred-pound woman I studied with, disarm a huge attacker by adding just enough movement to turn the oncoming force against itself. It is impressive!

Now imagine that instead of a physical blow coming at you, someone attacks you with a criticism or sarcastic remark. What are your options?

You could fight with them, adding force to the verbal exchange and escalating the conversation into an argument. You could flee by trying to ignore the remark or the person and hope that it will not return. Or perhaps you'll freeze in your tracks and the stories will begin to spin in your head, bringing up reactions that are all too familiar, but have never been resolved.

With fighting, you might convince yourself you're stronger than with fleeing or freezing, but don't be fooled. The more attention you give an opposing force, the stronger it becomes.

What might the forth option of *flowing* look like? Internally, you make a slight adjustment and move "off the line." Perhaps you tell yourself, "This isn't my stuff; it's theirs." Add just enough to disarm them. Try a sense of humor as a weapon. It's one of the greatest disarming tools of all time.

Return to your biggest opponent; the internal stories that you tell yourself. I'll take my own example of focusing on the single A-minus, rather than all the A's. When I hear that self-criticism come up inside of me, I say to myself, "Aha … there's my mom again! I think I'll just send her along on her way …." The act of *noticing* the voice is the self-awareness of tool number one, and sense of humor is the added energy to disarm the self-critical comment.

Let *sense of humor* be your ally in disarming those stories in your head!

Are you beginning to see how this works? While our hearts are whole, but often hidden away for protection, our head is much more complex. It has a "golden" side and a "shadow" side.[32] To best deal with our mind monsters, first use our self-

---

[32] Carl Jung introduced the notion of "shadows" and described the shadow to be the unknown dark side of the personality

awareness to *notice* that the story running in your head isn't serving your higher good.

Just as there are at least two sides to every story, there are two sides to your head component. There's the Magnificent golden side, aligning perfectly with your heart-sourced vision, reinforcing it, and you move forward with clear purpose. There's also your shadow side, creating the stories that hold your fears, self-doubt, and limiting beliefs.

There's a well-known story which describes this perfectly. It's about an old Cherokee who is teaching his grandson about life:

"A fight is going on inside me," he said to the boy.

"It is a terrible fight and it is between two wolves. One is evil—he is anger, envy, sorrow, regret, greed, arrogance, self-pity, guilt, resentment, inferiority, lies, false pride, superiority, and ego."

He continued, "The other is good—he is joy, peace, love, hope, serenity, humility, kindness, benevolence, empathy, generosity, truth, compassion, and faith. The same fight is going on inside you—and inside every other person too."

The grandson thought about it for a minute and asked his grandfather, "Which wolf will win?"

The old Cherokee replied, "The one you feed."

The mind is complex, and these core stories were created at a more formative time in your life when they served the purpose of protecting you. But as you grow up, they instead can become saboteurs to your own Magnificence.

Rather than attempt to slay them with force, freeze with non-action, or flee, learn to harness their power and use it in your life.

Cycling the Head and Heart

We'll summarize what we've covered with the MQformula before moving to its final component; intentional Action.

To obtain powerful action in the world in matters really important to us we need both tools—our self-awareness and our heart—to work *together*. As they cycle back and forth, your head and heart must communicate to sort through any confusion and stress, and reach a place of clarity and inner peace.

Observe how these mind monster stories fit into the rock-climbing belay analogy. It's your heart-sourced vision which carries your deepest passion that must lead the way in your life. If your heart and head—your passion and true purpose—are in alignment with one another, this vision continues to lead your life forward in a Magnificent manner. However, it's when your mind slips into its shadow side—the wolf that carries your fears, self-doubt, and limiting beliefs—that your heart begins to fall.

That's when your self-awareness needs to kick in. With flow and a sense of humor, you can "catch" your mind as it begins to feed those false beliefs and stories to your heart. Then, as it begins to fall out of alignment with your true purpose, compassionately notice and respond with, *"Aha! I see you, fear. I see you, self-doubt. I see you, limiting belief. You are trying to feed my mind and distract my heart."* Catch it with your self-awareness and send that story on its way!

It is *not* the real Magnificent you!

Always remember to have _compassion_ for yourself.

Above all else, remember to have *compassion* for yourself as your Watcher notices that trickster story attempting to distract your heart from its climb. Love yourself. Be kind to yourself. Don't try to fight back the story. Don't flee from it. Don't freeze when it shows up. Rather, simply *notice* it, acknowledge it as the old friend that wants to visit with you again. That old story has a life of its own which will never change; your job is simply to see it for what it is, recognize it no longer holds power over you, step aside and send it flowing along on its own way.

As Michael Singer describes in The Untethered Soul:

"Eventually you will see that the real cause of problem is not life itself. It's the commotion the mind makes about life that really causes the problems ... the only permanent solution to your problems is to go inside and let go of the part of you that seems to have so many problems with reality. Once you do that, you'll be clear enough to deal with what's left."

The real flow comes with the art of watching and noticing what arises within you (including your thoughts and emotions) and *letting go* of those stories which don't serve you. This is where some regular morning meditation or spiritual practice really has its most powerful effects. It's not in the isolation of meditation that the deepest work is done, but rather *applying* the practice of noticing to your experiences throughout your waking life.[33]

Notice on a more regular and conscious basis where you're slipping away from your heart and it becomes easier to return to that place of passionate engagement with your decisions and activities.

This is the perfect place to take a deep breath, pause and feel the power of your heart's energy and self-awareness working *together*. This is the passion-powered source that will serve you best in your life.

We've seen how it's possible to catch our heart from falling by combining this cycling process of **A**wareness in our head with our **H**eart-sourced vision. We continue this journey with the final MQformula component: powerful, intentional, passion-powered, purpose-driven **A**ction in the world.

---

[33] for a deeper understanding of this, both Eckart Tolle's The Power of Now and Michael Singer's The Untethered Soul are highly recommended.

CHAPTER 8:

Breaking Through to Powerful <u>A</u>ction

"Intention is the core of all conscious life. It is our intentions that create karma, our intentions that help others, our intentions that lead us away from the delusions of individuality toward the immutable verities of enlightened awareness. Conscious intention colors and moves everything."
–Master Hsing Yun

Finally, we come to the third component of the MQformula: intentional Action in the world. Everything else we've addressed means little in relation to the actual change that occurs in our personal behavior as we face those challenges in our lives, both small and large.

Keep in mind there are two forms of behavioral change—internal and external. The external are more obvious. Am I brave enough to ask this person out on a date? To overcome my fear and take this new job? To have that difficult conversation with my friend? To join the rock-climbing gym and learn to climb? To literally jump off this cliff on a hang-glider?

The internal changes are often subtle, but nevertheless real. They may show up as non-action rather than action. Patience is a great example. Can I exercise more patience when dealing with this person and *not* blow up at them? Can I sit quietly waiting for the results of my medical test and *not* feel overwhelming anxiety?

Deeper listening is another of these internal shifts. Can I develop the capacity to recognize that I talk too much and need to quiet my own mind and agenda so that I can really take in what the other person is saying? This example extends much further into the realm of recognizing your own preconceived notions and prejudices as well. Can I meet a person who is wearing a nose ring without judging them? Can I meet an elderly person and realize they're more than a crumpled body, and may contain great wisdom that I might learn?

Whether the challenges of your life manifest as more overt actions or subtler internal shifts, the third component of the MQformula remains the same; creating *intentional Action*. Each moment of each day we're faced with decisions both small and large. Sometimes these events are almost ridiculously humorous. For example, every time I go out to a restaurant and try to choose what I want, it's like a major life event. My internal dialogue sounds something like this:

> *This dish seems interesting, but what if I don't like it? What if Liz orders something that looks better and she won't let me taste it? I've ordered that before and it was delicious, so should I go for that sure bet, or be adventurous and try something different?*

We're constantly moving through our life. We have choices at each turn we take. Practicing the techniques of the MQformula—getting our head and heart to flow together—is an ongoing process we can practice mastering many times in a day.

Break the process down with the example of ordering from a menu. Perhaps there are two or three tempting choices confusing you. The exact same elements are at play here.

Your head is expressing its fears, self-doubt, and limiting beliefs which are contributing to covering up your heart-sourced vision.

In the case of what to order, fear might subconsciously be saying, *but what if it doesn't taste good?* Your self-doubt shows up in its obvious confusion of what to order. What about your limiting beliefs? Perhaps there is a part of you that believes that if the meal isn't perfect, all will be lost. Have you perhaps forgotten that a huge part of this planet's population has no food whatsoever in front of them at this very moment that you're laboring over your decision?

Step One of the MQformula is to *notice* all those things spinning in your head. Are they paralyzing you in some way? *Oh, no. Here comes the waitperson. I need to make a decision quickly!*

Take a breath. Notice your anxiety, your confusion, your paralysis. Maybe you came to the restaurant knowing in advance the perfect thing to order, but you're informed they're out of that. Now what? Notice your disappointment. Take another breath.

Listen to your heart, not your head.

What was your *intention* in going out to dinner? Was it to have the perfect meal? Or was it to enjoy the company of your partner? If they're out of your perfect dinner choice, or the meal was disappointing, you still have their company. Isn't that perfect *already?*

Perhaps you came in with the intention of trying something new and different from your past ordering patterns. If your meal ends up not tasting as good as anticipated, has anything been gained? Was it a waste, or can you take the fact that you were adventurous in ordering into account? After all, the idea of adventure is built around not knowing the exact results, isn't it? Sometimes it turns out as you had hoped, sometimes not. But you were bold enough to take action and try something new. Wasn't that in itself worth it?

It is our *heart-sourced intention* we must listen to, not the confusion of our minds. Noticing when we slip into the stories in our head is the first step of the process, whether small or large. Using our Watcher as an ally to see what thoughts and emotions occur is the main component of a regular practice of flowing through our actions in the world.

Once you begin to *let go* of getting caught up in the moment-to-moment story feeding your fears, self-doubt, and limiting beliefs, you will be freer to *listen to your heart*.

If your heart's intention is to be with your partner at dinner and the meal turns out disappointing, you're still in alignment with your *intended purpose,* which was to have a good time.

Maybe the restaurant was closed due to an unexpected flooding, so you ended up laughing about your expectations while you sat at a nearby fast-food place instead.

While this example of ordering food might seem small (and perhaps never an issue for you), it serves to illustrate the basic components of the MQformula process. You might be the type of person who knows what they like, orders the same thing every time, and is satisfied over and over again. Perhaps you don't care about adventure and trying new things. That's perfectly fine.

Judgments from others, or yourself, are not a part of this process. Remember: Never compare yourself to anyone else.

As we stated earlier, *"It's all good ... until it's NOT."* The MQformula will help you deal with those moments small or large in your life that are *not* going well. If all is flowing perfectly and you enjoy that same food repeatedly, then go for it! Life is intended to be joy-filled and full of love. It's in the falling of our hearts when that joy and love is often lost. If your life is full of those elements already, and you have inner peace and satisfaction with your life, carry on!

And, at some point or another in your life experience, there will no doubt be moments of challenge to face. It's in those times that your head and heart must work together in this relationship described in the MQformula. The art of this process is in practicing it regularly.

It's OK to notice when things are going well, and you are feeling joyful.

Those circumstances will feed your heart and strengthen your intention to make them happen more. I can think of no better example of this than my grandson, Otis, to whom this book is dedicated. Unfortunately, I live eleven hours away from him. That means that it's a challenge to spend time with him. When I finally do, my heart is overflowing. That reinforces my intention to create the circumstances to spend even more time with him. Yes, I absolutely notice when I miss him and feel disappointed that I'm not closer—and I'm taking slow but steady action steps in my decision-making to create more opportunities for us to be together.

> **Set your *intention* to create more heart-sourced decisions. Then focus your *attention* on doing exactly that.**

As I set my *intention* to create more heart-sourced decisions and focus my *attention* on acting in that direction, I'll eventually manifest the circumstances to fall into place according to that heart-sourced vision.[34]

However, until you can free yourself from those stories in your mind that keep you from this heart-sourced vision, you'll find yourself dwelling more on what you don't have, rather than what you can create.

---

[34] This is taken from the 3-part Passion Test formula, referenced earlier (Janet Bray Attwood): "Intention-Attention-No Tension"

> ***Gratitude*** **is an excellent practice**
> **for maintaining perspective.**

Many people use *gratitude* as a regular source of shifting their attention from the stories in their head to their appreciation of what *is* present in their life. Gratitude is an excellent tool to keep your heart nourished in challenging times. Others use positive affirmations and visualizations to stay centered and on-track with their heart-sourced vision.

Exercises for Breaking Through and Letting Go

Becoming aware of and breaking through (or letting go of) your fears, self-doubt, and limiting beliefs is the first critical step to a life created from intentional Action. Once that occurs, the space opens within you and your heart leads your climb to action. This powerful combination of self-awareness and of self-sabotaging stories with the power of your heart-sourced vision allows you to step into breakthrough intentional action.

In beginning *the practice of noticing* what's limiting and holding you back, you might need some additional tools to assist you. Here's a few of those, but keep in mind that the most powerful tool you already have is the ally of your Watcher—that part of you able to catch your heart from falling on its climb.

Our Fears (External Factors)

Take a closer look at one of the main things holding people back from moving forward in their life; fear. Much has been written on fear as our basic instinct developed since the time of the cave man. That "flight or fight" portion of our brain known as the amygdala plays a big part in our survival.

Yet the stories we add to that basic instinct can often magnify those fears unnecessarily.

> *"We suffer more often in imagination than in reality."*
> *-Seneca the Younger*

Tim Ferris, author of <u>The Four-Hour Work Week</u>, created an exercise he calls "fear-setting,"[35] He suggests taking your worst fears and putting them under a conscious microscope to examine what might actually go wrong if you take action. This process is broken down into three main steps: Define, Prevent and Repair. Here is Tim's basic technique:

EXERCISE FOR FEARS

DEFINE	PREVENT	REPAIR
1)		
2)		

---

[35] http://mindfulambition.net/fear-setting-tim-ferriss/ or direct original source: https://tim.blog/2017/05/15/fear-setting/

Find a piece of paper and spend five to ten minutes doing this exercise:

- What are your greatest (and yes, also your smallest) fears?
- Define them clearly. Spell them out in their scariest detail!
- What is the worst-case scenario that could happen?
- What steps could you take to prevent or reduce the likelihood of these happening?
- What could you do to repair the damage *if* the worst-case scenario were to occur?

By taking time to consciously write out and address your worst possible fears, you bring them into the open and they become less overwhelming. You look right at your mind monsters and stare them down! There are many excellent resources available, if you find that fear and paralysis is one of the primary modes holding you back.

This approach is powerful and helpful in *breaking through* our fears. But once again, of the above steps mentioned, the most critical of all is stepping back with your self-awareness and *noticing* that your fear is present and holding you back.

It's important to note that, although our fears may appear to come from external factors, they're often essentially contained within us. As an example, we may fear that we'll fail if we attempt to accomplish something out in the world. Yet looking more closely, isn't it really the internal factor of worrying about what others might think of that failure that's the true fear?

Our Self-Doubt (Internal factors)

Self-doubt is perhaps one of the most difficult aspects on non-action to pin down. As noted in earlier chapters, self-doubt can be sourced to our very earliest belief system, and was developed when we were children. When others don't have confidence in us, we take on their story and make it our own, believing on some subconscious level that we're not capable, or worthy, of certain things.

Self-doubt is not an easy challenge to overcome. When it exists, it lies at the very core of our being and isn't readily extracted. The opposite, self-worth, is what we're striving to reinforce by way of increasing our internal Magnificence Quotient.

Increasing our self-worth is at the core of our Magnificence Quotient.

The best tool we can use in slowly growing beyond our self-doubt is our self-awareness. Combine this specifically with noticing *where you doubt yourself*, and remember the number one rule of developing your Magnificence Quotient (MQ):
Never compare yourself to anyone else.

We most readily fall into the trap of reinforcing our self-doubt when we compare ourselves to others. There is no simple answer to doubting yourself. It appears to be one of the default settings built into us. So instead of falling into that trap, notice when it comes at you. When you doubt yourself, your heart is falling away from loving yourself. Self-doubt is the force that takes you away from self-love.

Picture instead that self-doubt as that fist coming at your very center and, as in the Aikido analogy, step aside. Laugh at it. The act of noticing it is the same as "stepping off the line." By noticing it, you *separate yourself* and begin to take its power away. By adding your sense of humor and laughing at it, you add just enough force to slightly change its direction and send it on its way. Self-doubt does not belong to you. It has no place in your life. Self-doubt be gone!

To assist you in shifting perspective, refer to Maureen Zappala's brilliant diagram of how our perceptions of ourselves can create and reinforce this self-doubt.[36]

In the first diagram below, we see that when we're plagued by self-doubt, we perceive the value of what we know (our "dot" or "stuff I know") as very insignificant. We fall into the trap of self-talk, comparing our "dot" with what we think other people perceive ("stuff they think I know"). We further reduce our own significance by comparing ourselves to the world of knowledge in general ("stuff I think everyone else knows").

From this perspective, our very self-worth becomes radically diminished. Our self-doubt takes hold of our very existence and even when we *do* know quite a bit about something, we don't believe or value that body of knowledge and experience. Again, this comes from the trap of comparing ourselves to others!

---

[36] Note: The images below and paraphrasing of content are from the book Pushing Your Envelope: How Smart People Defeat Self-Doubt and Live with Bold Enthusiasm by Maureen Zappala, published by Lexington Press, © 2018 by Maureen Zappala. Reprinted by permission. Do not reproduce without permission from Maureen Zappala, maureen@maureenz.com; www.maureenz.com

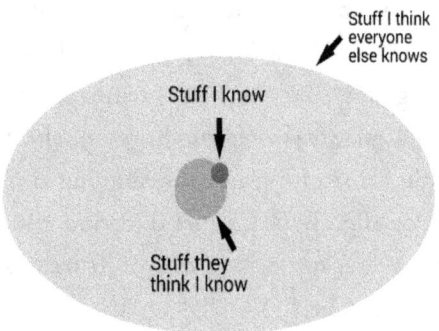

In its most radical form, this version of self-doubt affects even the most successful high-achievers and manifests itself as "The Imposter Syndrome"—a psychological pattern in which an individual doubts their accomplishments and has a persistent internalized fear of being exposed as a "fraud."[37] If you hold any level of self-doubt at all, this is very common, so relax and know that you're in good company.

To shift this perspective, try instead to view your "dot" ("the stuff I know") in the following manner:

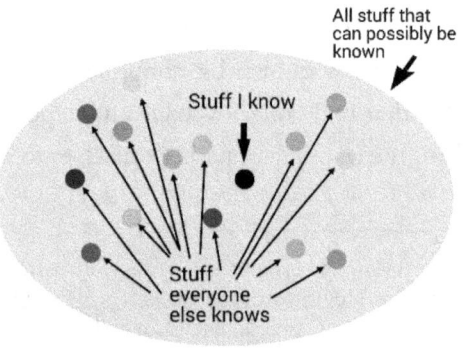

---

[37] https://en.wikipedia.org/wiki/Impostor_syndrome

In other words, each of us is a unique (and Magnificent!) "dot" in the universe with our own knowledge base and perspective. *Once we stop comparing ourselves to others, we realize that each of us has our own role to play—and knowledge to share—that is truly unique.*

EXERCISE FOR SELF-DOUBT

Take a few minutes to list out the things that make YOU unique. What have you experienced that no one else has? What perspective have you seen that others might benefit from? This might look like a body of knowledge that you have gained over time, or possibly an experience that you went through in your life that others might not even imagine. Perhaps this is something recent, or possibly dating back to your own childhood.

Make a list of a few of those experiences, areas of knowledge or characteristics that make you unique:

_____

_____

_____

_____

- Where have you come from that is unique to you?
- What experiences have you been through that no one else has?
- What makes you different, unique and special?

Shift your perspective from a place of comparing your "dot" to what you believe others might think, and all that you believe you don't know, to something different. Value yourself. Stay focused on your uniqueness. Be grateful that all experiences that brought you to this very place are exactly what have been necessary to create the unique and Magnificent being that you are. Recognize that you have something no one else has, and that others might benefit from your sharing your experience.

This is a great start to reducing your self-doubt and increasing your self-worth, not to mention your self-confidence, which you'll need when it's time for you to step up and act. If it speaks to you, try journaling, and stay on the path of *not comparing yourself to others*.

Our Limiting Beliefs (Overall factors)

Before we can break out, or let go, of our limiting beliefs, we must once again *notice* them. This is the irony of limiting beliefs; we can't always see them for ourselves. They show up in so many subtle ways that they become invisible. We surround ourselves with people who reinforce those same limiting beliefs and make them even more powerful.

There are countless examples of limiting beliefs, perhaps one of the most often referenced being breaking the four-minute mile. No one believed it could be done until Roger Bannister accomplished this in 1954. Since that time others have shaved an additional fifteen plus seconds from that record. New discoveries in science break the limits of our thinking regularly, because that *is* one of the jobs of science—to stretch the limits of what we know.

Apply this to our own thinking. Who says that I'm not capable of achieving amazing, outrageous, Magnificent things? Of writing books? Of rock climbing starting at the age of sixty? Of changing careers? Of breaking through money barriers that I never dreamed I could achieve? Always remember, however, that the first step in breaking through limiting beliefs, just as in dealing with fears, is the act of *noticing* them.

EXERCISE FOR LIMITING BELIEFS

In Chapter Four, we referenced Byron Katie's "The Work" and those four powerful questions you can ask yourself about the limiting beliefs that may be holding you back. We can't do justice to those powerful questions in one short exercise, but we can at least point to the power of this work. Take a few minutes to identify a belief you're holding about an incident with another person that you recently experienced. Perhaps some anger or resentment with someone, because you feel they've wronged you in some way.

Write a few words about that incident here:

_____

_____

_____

_____

Now ask yourself each of Byron Katie's four questions:

1. Is it true? (i.e. is this thought true?) ___Yes ___No

2. Can you *absolutely* know that it's true? (i.e. can I absolutely know this thought is true?)
___Yes ___No

3. How do you react when you believe that thought? (for example, what other thoughts or beliefs may come up because of this? How do you *feel* when you believe this is true about the person?)

_____

_____

_____

4. Who would you be without that thought?

_____

_____

_____

Take a moment to really reflect on the last question. Imagine, as hard as it might be for you if you're holding anger or resentment with a person, that you rid yourself of those thoughts. Do you see the sheer *power* we sometimes allow ourselves to be overcome by? You might even be right about the circumstances, while they were dead wrong. It doesn't really matter.

What matters is the power you allow the stories in your head to continue holding over you.

The moment you give your power away to the importance of those thoughts, you've lost the battle. Your thoughts will continue to spin, then your emotions will kick in even stronger, sending you into a tail-spin guaranteed to be counterproductive.

Such stories exist on many different levels. They're not just about other people. They are about core limiting beliefs each of us holds. Take the example of money and the power it wields over so many of us. If you grew up in a poor or struggling household (or at least if that was the mentality of the experience you had), then your limiting beliefs about money may run deeper than you can imagine. Those might include beliefs such as:

- Making money must be difficult
- Having an abundance of money will never be possible for me
- People who are born into families with lots of money don't deserve it
- People who have lots of money are naturally greedy
- It's not possible to have lots of money and be a genuine, caring person

These beliefs run so deep they often remain at the edge of our consciousness where they affect our behavior in subtle yet powerful ways. The point here is, once again, to *notice* and become more *self-aware* of those hidden beliefs driving our behavior. As described earlier, we often develop these beliefs at a very impressionable young age and hold on to them without even realizing it.

Becoming self-aware of our fears, self-doubt, and limiting beliefs is only the first step.

While being self-aware of our fears, self-doubt, and limiting beliefs is a great start, it's not enough to change our lives. We must not only *wake up* to these mind monsters, we must *step up and act* if our lives are to become truly Magnificent. With clear, powerful heart-sourced Action as our intention, we'll look at a few more auxiliary tools to supplement the major components of self-awareness and our passion-powered, heart-sourced vision.

CHAPTER 9:

More Action Tools for Your Journey

Start with A Single Step

Remember the nail in the barn? It was *one nail*, not the Olympic nail-driving competition. Whatever your challenge is, take it one small step at a time. That's how I approached rock climbing, at age fifty-nine, when I first walked into the new climbing gym that opened near my house. *How could those people possible dare to do what they are doing?* While part of me was fascinated, part of me froze. But I took the first small step by signing up to join. Then the helpful folks at the gym educated me. I hooked up to the auto-belay above and started to climb … just ten or fifteen feet at first.

"Now let go," Tommy said to me.

"You mean just LET GO?!" I repeated.

"Yes, it will catch your fall. Just let go."

And I did. I've been climbing since that time and I love it![38] Each step I progress, fear continues to resurface. Yet each time, I take it one small step further as I continue to build my level of self-confidence. I don't compare myself to the other climbers; instead, I focus on how far I've come, where I am at this moment,

---

[38] For a more vivid description, visit the authors blog at: www.MQfactor.com

and pushing through my fear, self-doubt, and limiting beliefs so I'll be able to make it to the next small level of accomplishment. That doesn't mean I don't interact, watch and learn from those more experienced climbers. It means I refuse to beat myself up over which skill-set level I "should" have accomplished at any given time.

Isn't that true for everything? Just take it one small action step at a time. It sounds simple, but unfortunately that's not always the case. Until you begin to consciously *notice* what's holding you back, what you're avoiding and doubting about yourself, and what fears and limiting beliefs you're holding, no real action steps will occur.

Tools, Tools, Tools

The word "tool" by definition typically refers to *"a device or implement, especially one held in the hand, used to carry out a particular function."* Tool can also refer to a concept, such as *"Creativity is the tool which allow a child's mind to grow."*[39] Here we are using it metaphorically to describe a method of taking powerful action in the world.

In our context, anything which can be used to further advance or accelerate the progress you make in manifesting your Magnificence can be referred to as a tool. The central components of the MQformula have also been referred to as the key tools of (1) self-awareness and (2) accessing your heart-sourced (passion-based) vision. Aligned together in the right

---

[39] http://www.businessdictionary.com/definition/tool.html

relationship, these two components result in intentional purpose-driven *Action in the world.*

The MQformula's two key tools are:
(1) Self-awareness and (2) Heart-sourced (passion-based) vision

German philosopher, Martin Heidegger described tools as being either "present-at-hand" or "ready-to-hand."[40] Basically, a tool can be lying in your toolbox as an object with its *potential* for service, but until it moves into its ready-to-hand action mode, nothing occurs:

A ready-to-hand entity, such as a tool, is *when it fits into a meaningful network of purposes and functions, i.e. when it becomes part of a world of practice.*[41]

After my bout with botulism, the hammer I picked up moved into an active state as I headed to the barn. I readied myself and consciously held my intention to act on something as I walked to the barn, not even knowing quite what the task was at that point.

Once I saw the nail sticking out of the post, my reason for picking up that hammer became clear to me. I had to accomplish *something* to feel better about myself. To someone looking from the outside in, that single nail might not have seemed a very large task, but given my circumstances, it was truly Magnificent.

The beauty of tools is that you can collect as many as you want! And yet, until you pick them up and put them to use, they

---

[40] Being and Time (Sein und Zeit)
[41] http://compendium.kosawese.net/term/present-at-hand-vorhanden-and-ready-to-hand-zuhanden/

are objects waiting for their potential to manifest. The same could be said of you.

Here's a review of some tools mentioned earlier that assist in supporting the "key tools" of self-awareness and our heart-sourced energy. Whether these additional tools are used to cultivate those two components, or to break through or let go of those things *blocking* your potential for Magnificence, makes no difference.

- Mindfulness and meditation practices of many kinds
- The Passion Test (Janet Bray Attwood)
- Fear-setting (Tim Ferris)
- The Four Questions from The Work (Byron Katie)
- The art of Aikido

What's important is to find the tools or methods that resonate with *you*.

This list could be expanded to dozens of different methods you can explore. For example, The Sedona Method[42] is a simple technique by which a person can learn to release unwanted emotions and other stressful factors. What's important is to find the tools or methods that resonate with *you,* and you begin to practice and cultivate them to better access those key components of self-awareness and your heart-sourced energy.

Whatever tools you choose to use, there are *three underlying elements* foundational to these methods referenced in the previous sections:

---

[42] https://www.sedona.com

- Compassion (for yourself and others)
- Gratitude
- Sense of humor

What's slightly different about these elements from other "tools" is that they're not in themselves a method, but more of an attitude, perspective or viewpoint from which you utilize the other tools in your toolbox.

Think of that same hammer which could be used in many ways. Besides building or doing something constructive, it could be used to destroy or hurt. This is true with any tool not used properly. The *intention* which you set is critical to manifesting your Magnificence.

If you flavor this intention with *gratitude*, *compassion* and a *sense of humor* as your core perspective, the attention you give to what you experience will result in actions building your Magnificence Quotient, not break it down or destroy it.

Love yourself first (have compassion for yourself). Practice gratitude for what *is*. Use your sense of humor to disarm all that does not serve you.

Daily Practice

"When you are clear, what you want will show up in your life ... and only to the extent that you are clear."
—Janet Bray Attwood

We spoke in earlier chapters about meditation and other mindful practices. Every person is different, so there's no one-size-fits-all way in which to center yourself and continue to develop self-awareness and mindfulness skills.

For many, meditation is the key. For others, a daily walk might accomplish the same thing. There are many beautiful practices to consider making a part of your regular life, such as yoga, exercise, martial arts, or whatever speaks to you.

What is key is that you find something that is a *routine daily practice*, a ritual of some sort.

Tony Robbins, for example, has a regular routine each morning to center himself and awaken fresh to life each day. His ritual includes meditation, thoughts focusing on gratitude, visualization of what he wants to accomplish that day, plus a plunge into 56 degree water to wake up all his senses and test his limits each morning!

Personally, I don't take that cold-water pool plunge, but I do wake up each day with a regular meditation, combining a series of breathing and tapping exercises, followed by time on the treadmill. Do some days vary due to an excessive crazy schedule, an early morning appointment or perhaps even sleeping in late? Yes, sometimes. Do I beat myself up about this? No. Remember, kindness and compassion toward yourself is key. As Don Miguel Ruiz says in The Four Agreements, *"Always do your best."* That's all you can do.

There is power in daily ritual. Selfish as it may appear on the surface at times, if you don't serve yourself first, what good will you be to serve others? Remember, that's why the instructions on the airplane say to put the oxygen mask on yourself first. You owe it to yourself to be strong, centered and healthy, so that ultimately you can serve others.

If you do not serve yourself first, what good will you be to serve others?

The power of developing and practicing some form of daily ritual for yourself can't be emphasized enough.[43] No matter what you choose, what matters most is to experience the quietness that releases what may be vibrating within you, and to step away from your thinking enough to "see yourself" in a different perspective.

For us to break through our limiting beliefs, we must transcend them in some way. To do this, we must first let go of all that holds us back. But letting go isn't just an intellectual exercise; it must be felt in some way in your body to truly be released. A few deep cleansing breaths, as is often the practice at the start of a yoga session, can serve to do this. Sometimes when I feel a lot of tension, anger or energy in my body as I sit down to meditate, I cup my hands together (one palm up and the other down) and shake them vigorously and repeatedly at my center (by my navel) for as long as necessary before they naturally slow down and the energy is released from my body. This is a small practice which I picked up studying Aikido, the peaceful martial art developed by Osensei ("Great Teacher").[44]

---

[43] A great read for understanding and practicing such rituals is Your Hidden Riches: Unleashing the Power of Ritual to Create a Life of Meaning and Purpose by Janet Bray Attwood and Chris Attwood.

[44] https://en.wikipedia.org/wiki/Morihei_Ueshiba

Whatever your ritual is, commit to it daily.

For some people, their ritual comes at night with a mental summary of all that happened during the day and a focus on gratitude. Some choose to do both, or to stop in the middle of the day for a short time to regain their center and sense of calm. Experiment and find what works best for you.

As you go about your day, remember to practice *noticing* with your Watcher. What works best for you, and what doesn't? Don't over-think anything. Notice the point at which you suddenly begin to lose patience or get frustrated. Take a breath. Be kind to yourself.

The real power of daily ritual such as meditation doesn't come during the isolated act itself. The full potential and mastery of practice is incorporating the depth of that quietness into your day, especially in the middle of stress and chaos. But without first developing the capability of self-awareness to catch yourself falling into that chaos, you're destined instead to become a victim of daily drama.

Remember our end goal: to experience the flow of life with its fullest joy and inner peace. *"It's all good ... until it's not."* That's when your self-awareness and heart-sourced vision will be ready-to-hand to serve you best. Practice and cultivate these during quiet, calm times so that you can access them whenever needed.

CHAPTER 10:

Mission, Passion and Purpose

"A mission statement is not something you write overnight... But fundamentally, your mission statement becomes your constitution, the solid expression of your vision and values. It becomes the criterion by which you measure everything else in your life."
-Stephen Covey

Before we lay out the entirety of the MQformula, we'll address one more way of consciously understanding how to align your head and heart: Mission.

When your head and heart are truly working together, your stress, anxiety and lack of self-confidence will fall away. Recall, however, that we spent a great deal of time discussing how our mind can play tricks on us. Those stories that block our Magnificence seem to return again and again at the most inopportune times, resulting in confusion rather than clarity.

To this end, we can utilize the concept of Mission. There's also a formula for creating a Mission, which looks like this:

Vision + Action = Mission

We've already discussed both vision and action. Vision in its truest sense is that which is heart-sourced. The passion and power of this heart-sourced vision is what helps us break through our fears, self-doubt, and limiting beliefs to create Action in the world. By consciously forming a mission, we use that to check ourselves in times of confusion. As the above quote from Stephen Covey notes, creating a mission can be a lifelong process. Here, we're going to do a basic exercise to begin crafting that statement. Although simplified, it's a starting point from which you can continue to build and modify until it becomes an expression of *your* vision and values.

EXERCISE FOR CREATING MISSION[45]

Close your eyes for a few moments, listen to your heart, and picture an ideal world where there is no conflict or stress of any kind. How would you describe that world?

To assist you, here's a sample list of possible adjectives that might be applicable to your vision. Go ahead and circle two or three of those that you resonate with, or write in others not on the list:

Loving Abundant Peaceful Cooperative Supportive Vibrant Compassionate Adventurous Courageous Respectful Trusting Generous Passionate Creative

---

[45] The author's version of this formula for mission is taken from his learnings working for 16 years in The Mankind Project, including his role as International Mission Co-Coordinator (including 14 countries) for that organization from 2009-2012.

MISSION, PASSION AND PURPOSE

Now that you have those adjectives, close your eyes again and picture what activities are going on in this perfect world. What are the people in your vision *doing* to make that type of world? What are *you* doing to help create that picture? Again, here is a sample list of some of those possibilities. Add your own. What might you be doing to create such a world?

Caring   Nurturing   Loving   Supporting   Teaching
Inspiring   Creating   Learning   Listening   Guiding
Sharing   Connecting

Circle or write in two or three of those activities that you might do from your heart-sourced place.

Now combine the two or three words from the first section with those activities and fill in the blanks below:

I co-create a _____, _____ **and**
_____ **world by** _____,
_____ **and** _____.

Here are a couple of examples:

*I co-create a loving, peaceful and compassionate world
by caring, nurturing and teaching.
I co-create an abundant, generous and cooperative world
by sharing, connecting and listening.*

Try to keep your statement short, simple and powerful. After ten years of forming and reforming my personal mission statement, I finally got it simplified to nine words:

I co-create a vibrant world by inspiring people's Magnificence!

Why is this exercise important? Because it brings powerful, conscious intention to your way of being in the world. This conscious intention brings clarity to your *purpose* and keeps your actions in line with your mission if you use it as a guide to remind you.

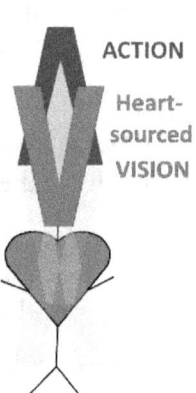

PURPOSE
That area of overlap where your Actions are in alignment with your heart-sourced Vision is where you MAKE A DIFFERENCE in the world!
This is your higher Purpose.

ACTION

Heart-sourced VISION

As an example of this, I'll share a simple shift that I experienced while setting this intention to keep my mission as a daily guide. One day I returned to my office to find that my administrative assistant had made a terrible mistake on a task. I began to reprimand her, but as I felt myself starting to react, I *noticed* that I was about to lose it. I stepped back in that small moment of self-awareness, took a breath, and repeated my guiding mission statement in my mind, asking myself, *"Are you really inspiring either your own Magnificence or hers by reacting this way?"*

The clear answer was No. In that moment, I was able to reframe my interaction, and instead focus on what could be done differently next time to avoid that mistake. My mission statement was a conscious reminder to keep me on track. It's another tool to align conscious, intentional action with our passion and purpose.

The MQformula already contains the elements of mission: Vision and Action. Experiment with a mission that speaks to your heart, your vision of the world that you would like to create, and what your action in that world might look like. Make it simple and powerful. Put it in your toolbox and pull it out as a reminder whenever you need it. *Make a difference in this world!*

CHAPTER 11:

The MQformula — Putting It All Together

"Aah ... to point a finger at the moon!
But whoa to those who take the finger for the moon."
- Zen saying

We've covered a lot of territory in describing the key components of the MQformula, all designed to cultivate our internal MQ, or Magnificence Quotient. At the same time, it's important to remember the formula is simply a tool—a pointer—to gain perspective and create shifts in our life when things aren't working well.

To the extent that we pick this tool up and use it, we increase the possibility of turning stressful and difficult moments into joyous and peaceful ones. By using the MQformula's components, we increase the *possibility* of shifting our behavior and being more open to aha moments. It's within those moments that our sense of inner peace and joy—along with our internal Magnificence—reveals itself.

To recap and remember more easily, we'll put all of this into a visual formula. But before we do, I'll add a brief disclaimer/footnote on the word "formula."

"Formula" typically implies a mathematical or scientific approach—a proven, tested method applied over and over again which will always produces the same guaranteed results. Wikipedia states:

> *"In a general context, formulas are applied to provide a mathematical solution for real world problems ... Some may be general ... other formulas may be specially created to solve a particular problem."*

Merriam-Webster's dictionary *describes "a conventionalized statement intended to express some fundamental truth or principle especially as a basis for negotiation or action."*

The use of the word formula in this context may spark some judgment or reaction in some critical way; if so, first *notice* that reaction. The awareness of your reaction will point you to a deeper level of your belief system, which is exactly what I'm referring to in this exploration.

If you're of a scientific bent, where the goal is typically to prove something certain, you probably won't find that certainty here. However, if you let go of the desired result of certainty and instead focus on the process of discovery itself, you're in the right place.

If you live life from more of a spiritual, religious or sacred perspective, don't lose faith based on the use of this word. Formula—like the word "God"—is just a word ... a pointer. Just as a flashlight is intended to shine the light on something to reveal more of it, the MQformula moves and guides us in a direction ... a method to shine the light on our own Magnificence.

THE MQFORMULA — PUTTING IT ALL TOGETHER

Now for an even closer look.

Awareness — **H**eart — **A**ction

Self-Awareness + Heart-Sourced Vision + Intentional Action
= Magnificent Moment (AHA!)

$$A+H+A = MQ$$

For those with a more analytical mind who want to refine this formula even further (this is optional):

$$[(A \times H) + A = MQ^2]$$

Why A x H? Because the Awareness and Heart-sourced components must *cycle back and forth,* playing off one another until we can sort through what's real (our conscious and intentional purpose) from the *story* in our head containing the seeds of fear, self-doubt, and limiting beliefs. Recall this diagram from Chapter 7:

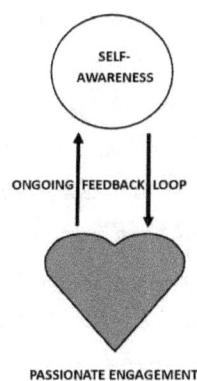

This first portion of the formula must sometimes repeat itself over and over until our heart-sourced vision is powerful enough to either break through or let go of what holds us back. It's because of this cycling process we can *move to action in the world.* Adding that action, whether an external act or an internal shift in our behavior, results in our increased MQ.

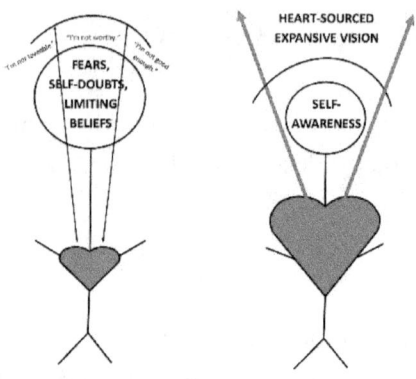

Why MQ^2 (squared)? Because our Magnificence is powerful! It's magnified in our smallest of magnificent moments. It's in those small, enlightened aha moments that we shine! As Marianne Williamson so beautifully put it:

"Our deepest fear is not that we are inadequate. Our deepest fear is that we are powerful beyond measure. It is our light, not our darkness that most frightens us. We ask ourselves, who am I to be brilliant, gorgeous, talented, fabulous? Actually, who are you not to be? You are a child of God. Your playing small does not serve the world. There is nothing enlightened about shrinking so that other people won't feel insecure around you. We are all meant to shine,

as children do. We were born to make manifest the glory of God that is within us. It's not just in some of us; it's in everyone. And as we let our own light shine, we unconsciously give other people permission to do the same. As we are liberated from our own fear, our presence automatically liberates others."

Truly, *magnificent moments* are about those instances of awakening within each of us as individuals. They're unique to us as a reflection of where we've come from, where we stand in this moment, and what we need to do to move forward and push through our self-doubts, fears, and self-limiting beliefs. The sole measure is the comparison of our previous self with the self we uncover and reveal in that aha moment.

This capacity to push through into our own Magnificence is the truest measure of our self-worth, not the comparison to—or criticism from—anyone else.

Each of us is a diamond in the rough. At each moment we consciously choose to access our heart-sourced vision, we move forward in our unique life and take one step closer to becoming the Magnificent self that we're each destined to be.

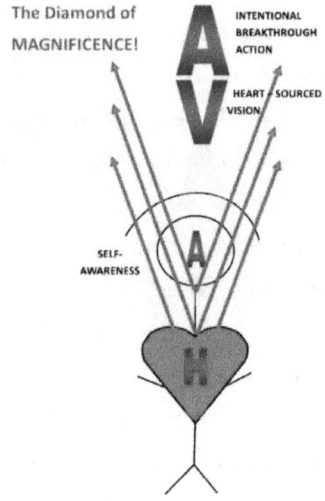

Yet that single step can often seem insurmountable, because we tend to be masters at holding ourselves back from our own greatest shining light. Now that we've broken down all the elements of this formula, take one final look at the process as a whole.

CHAPTER 12:

Nail Your Magnificence!

"Many people think excitement is happiness.... But when you are excited you are not peaceful. True happiness is based on peace."
-Thich Nhat Hanh

So, what do we *do* with this MQformula? What difference might it really make in our lives? What is the end game? Review the basics for a moment before addressing this practical question.

First and foremost, remember to *never compare yourself with anyone else.* Take that essential element of your Magnificence Quotient with you. As well as not comparing yourself to other people, this also applies to yourself. If you judge that you might have done better with a task, that judgment is really rooted in a perception of a you that is other than present. It may be a you of the past *("I used to be able to do this much better.")* or a you of the future *("I'll never be able to finish this book or climb that mountain.")* Essentially, have compassion for where you *are in the present*. Be grateful for who you are and for what you *do* have, rather than focus on who you are not or what you don't have. You are beautiful, unique ... yes, even Magnificent! Take that in and bless yourself in all of its perfect imperfection, as that may be.

Second, *remember the basics.* Cultivate your Watcher. Become aware of your different states of mind, of your thoughts and emotions as they arise. They show up for a reason, even though we may not understand what that reason is. Again, *be compassionate* as you observe yourself. Remember to *smile* at yourself. Make it a game, if need be. Develop this ability to step away from yourself in good and joyous times on a regular basis, so that your Watcher "muscle" can show up reflexively during the dark and dangerous moments when your heart begins to fall from the side of the cliff. By doing this, you'll be able to "belay" that which is truly important ... the power and passion stored in your heart.

> **Make a game of stepping back and looking at yourself with compassion and a sense of humor.**

Third, *open your heart.* Once you have caught yourself from falling, take a few breaths. Again, compassion for yourself is critical. Begin with turning that fabulous and powerful loving energy of your heart upon yourself, so that you'll be strong enough to eventually serve others. Don't be afraid to dig deep into your heart's memories for things that brought you joy in the past and revisit those. Maybe you recall from a distance the wonder and joy of painting as a child. *Listen to your heart.* If your fears, self-doubt, and self-limiting beliefs start to crop up around the idea of you painting, *notice* that. Step away from those stories running in your head about never being a great painter. Smile and laugh about your doubts and fears. Put them out in front of you and move on to the most critical step.

Go sign up for a class. *Take conscious and intentional action* to follow what's tugging at your heart. *Listen to your inner passions.* Whether it's an obvious one like learning to paint, or a less obvious one such as how much better you might feel by becoming a more patient person, the important thing is to *do something*. We are here on this earth for such a short time. Ask yourself how you would feel if you were to die and not experience the things that your doubts and fears keep from you. As Tony Robbins reminds us:

"It is in your moments of decision that your destiny is shaped."

Aligning Your Head and Heart

The elements of the MQformula essentially create integrity between the relationship of your head and heart. Learning to sweep away your fears, self-doubt, and limiting beliefs is a clearing process to unblock the channel between your head and heart. It's literally only about eighteen inches from one to the other, yet it often can feel like the greatest distance on Earth.

Mahatma Ghandi once said,

*"Happiness is when what you think,
what you say, and what you do are in harmony."*

When our thoughts, our words, and our actions are all in alignment, we have *integrity* within ourselves. To achieve such internal peace and harmony, you must be true to yourself. Developing your self-awareness and consistently *noticing* what is happening within you with respect to your thoughts and emotions is the first step. Pushing through these thoughts—or, ideally, letting go of them—follows this self-awareness. Then, finally, once you've distanced yourself from all the voices not truly yours, dive deeper into your heart-sourced vision and reconnect with what *you* truly want.

I recently ran across a young friend who had just broken off an engagement. The story and details don't matter. What is significant is that she hadn't been able to tell anyone about it. My sense is that she had a lot of confusion and shame around ending the engagement. She acknowledged being caught up in what everyone else was expecting of her, including her mother, whom she knew was anxious to have grandchildren. The pressure and voices of her family, friends and society's expectations of what she *should* be doing were completely blocking what she knew in her heart was the right thing to do.

To create a Magnificent life, we must become firmly grounded in our own heart-sourced vision and beliefs. That means sorting out and separating the voices that aren't ours from those that truly come from within us. Once we access the power of our own heart and the *real* vision we want for ourselves, we can then set the *intention* to follow that and, when the moment comes, take the *intentional action* step true to our own heart.

Our task is to sweep away the clutter of other people's beliefs and find our own truth about ourselves. Once we accomplish this, our head and heart align with one another. This is the ultimate path to true happiness.

Claim Your POWER

You can observe, notice and theorize all day long, but the key to a fully actualized life lies in the *action steps* you take. The alignment of our head and heart allows us to be internally at peace. However, until we *act* on our heart-sourced vision, nothing will really change in our lives. This is the third and critical component of the AHA formula that will manifest your passion and purpose, and result in a real impact in your life and the lives of others.

You, as an individual, must take full responsibility for creating results to shift your world. Awakened to your internal processes, you can't blame others or external circumstances. Yes, those circumstances may be difficult or perhaps unfair on some level. However, you always have a *choice* in the matter. Your response to external circumstances remains in your control and is the *only* thing that matters.

As concentration camp survivor Victor Frankl puts it in Man's Search for Meaning, *"The last of the human freedoms is the ability to choose one's attitude in any given set of circumstances."*

Whether your action involves shifting your internal attitude in a quiet manner, or by more audibly speaking up and taking clear, observable action in the world, you are responsible for claiming your power in this life.

You are responsible for claiming your power in this life!

Using the MQformula in Daily Life

Can I really get a *guarantee* that following the MQformula steps will bring me either small or large aha moments in my life?

Some time ago, I mailed a package to my daughter in New York. I sent it priority mail with an acknowledgement of delivery to be sent back to me. I don't even recall what it was; but it was for my daughter who is one of the most important people in my life and I wanted to be sure it arrived safely. Well, it didn't. In fact, what should have taken about three days to get there turned into well over ten days with still no sign of arrival. I was quite upset, so I went into the main post office with my receipt and demanded to know why that package hadn't been delivered.

"Can't you track where it is?" I asked the woman behind the counter.

"We can let you know when it's delivered, but that's all," she replied.

"For crying out loud," I said. "My daughter can tell me when it arrives, and it hasn't yet. That's why I am standing here! Isn't this guaranteed?"

The woman, perhaps in her late sixties with curly graying hair, had a weathered yet wise look about her. She peered at me over her reading glasses and said, "Sonny, there are no guarantees in life."

I stood there staring at her. At first, I couldn't believe it. Something inside of me suddenly shifted. Somehow, I knew that she was right. Her words seemed to magically melt my anger. I have no idea what that woman had been through in her life, but I had the sense that it was a *lot* … that those few words she shared with me in that moment were learned and earned from some very hard lessons ... that this package I was pouring so much of my emotional energy into paled in comparison to what she had gone through over the years.

I felt the anger just leave my body as I looked back at her and said, "Well, I guess you may be right about that. Thank you for your help checking on it." Her statement was a simple yet profound truth that has stuck with me ever since—a small aha moment that reminds me nothing in life is guaranteed. Just a day later, after I had let go of all that anger and frustration, my daughter called to say she had finally received it.

I can't take credit, in that moment at the post office, for catching myself as my heart fell into frustration and anger. Instead, I owe a debt of gratitude to that woman behind the counter for acting as my Watcher. I wasn't the one who caught myself from falling into a deeper anger. It was this woman's sense of peace that pervaded and somehow spoke to my heart, resulting in the dissipation of my own anger. It was she who was serving to belay my heart—catching me from falling with her profound wisdom. She saw my frustration and anger, and helped belay my heart.

Sometimes things fall that way. Others can see us better than we can see ourselves. Once we begin to watch and notice our various states, we become more open to receiving useful observations from others. Remember, our Watcher muscle is a tool in our toolbox. If I were working on a big carpentry project, I might want an assistant to hold the hammer for a moment. And so it is with our Watcher. The important part is to smile and be compassionate with ourselves.

Don't resist the truth when it shows up.

You will know it, whether it comes from your own noticing, or the watchfulness of a friend. Sometimes this comes from a stranger. It doesn't matter what the source is or who gets the credit for noticing. *What matters is that you catch your heart from falling into those dark places.* That you *open your heart and listen to it.* And finally, that you *act on it.* Again, this may be obvious external action in the world or it may be an internal shift to a more peaceful place.

What does this have to do with the MQformula and our everyday world? The MQformula is intended to move us into action. The only guarantee we can have is the promise to ourselves to utilize these tools to the best of our ability. This movement or shift in our consciousness can initially remain internal, but eventually will manifest into our external interaction with others. We may go out and decide to climb all the highest mountains in the world, as a friend of mine literally did over the span of twenty years.[46] Or, we may shift and become a more patient or loving individual. This result will ultimately manifest in our actions or a choice of non-action (such as the non-violent civil disobedience that Ghandi displayed).

Will we become enlightened beings? Perhaps ... for just a moment. Must we always struggle through life? That's a choice each of us gets to make in every moment. Now with the MQformula you have some options. Use it. When the struggles

---

[46] Visit the author's website:
http://whatmademethink.com/2015/04/10/what-made-me-think/

occur, and your inner peace and joy recede to the background—when your heart begins to fall—pull out your toolbox. Remember your heart-sourced intention and purpose. Notice the struggle. Breathe. Be compassionate to yourself. Take the world and yourself lightly. Be grateful. Laugh at what's going on.

What Does Love Have To Do With It?

Make no mistake about it. Although we have spent much time talking about what goes on in our heads, the core of our Magnificence lies in our hearts and our natural passions. The MQformula is a process designed to return to this core. The word love has barely been used in this exposé of the head-heart dilemma with all its confusion, struggle and tension in our lives. Yet love is the source of our natural energy and the root of our passions.

Love is the source of our passions.

Plain and simply put, if we could remain acting from a place of love in this world, we wouldn't have the tensions and struggles we create. And, diving even deeper, it's the *love for ourselves* that can truly be the most difficult task of all to practice.

The MQformula is a practical reminder—a method—to utilize at any moment to clear away the clutter in our head and reveal the wondrous and yes, Magnificent, heart each of us holds at our center. Keep things as simple as you can. We've spent a good deal of time doing exercises to recall and reveal the source and power that the stories in our head contain. This is necessary for us to understand where we go off-track in our lives. But ultimately, we must return to the real source—our hearts.

One More Thing

One last note on use of the MQformula. At first, you may have to separate the components. Practice noticing and watching regularly throughout your day. This is key to uncluttering the stories in your head leading you astray. Don't think about diving into your heart. That's not a thought process anyway. Just focus on practicing and cultivating your Awareness about what is present in your head and how that's affecting you.

Then, as a separate practice, consciously set aside some quiet time to listen to your heart and *feel* it. You may be so busy that you must designate special time just to clear a space for your heart to breathe. For many, yoga serves as an exercise for the body and centering for the heart.

Over time, your Awareness will begin to function on a real-time basis. Instead of looking back and reflecting on situations that didn't go so well, your Watcher will begin to be present *during* your experiences. Time will almost seem as if it's slowing down, and your Watcher will gradually become increasingly present.

The process of the MQformula will seem to compress and become more reflexive. Recall the story of Jake starting to blow up in anger at his girlfriend, then suddenly becoming aware and catching himself. His heart was falling out of love. His awareness caught him, and he returned to his corrected path of action.

NAIL YOUR MAGNIFICENCE!

Awareness — **H**eart — **A**ction

AHA!

Go out and practice these three steps. Don't over-analyze. Live. Make mistakes. Be aware of their effect on you. Love. Climb. Fall. Catch yourself. Climb again. Fall again. It's okay.

Love yourself first, so your love will overflow and be shared with others. Be compassionate. Be grateful. Laugh at yourself. Forgive. Be kind to others. Life is short. Feel it from the depths of your heart. Dive deep. Love, laugh, listen and learn.

You are a miracle of head and heart. Use them together to serve both yourself and the world.

> *May your thoughts be full of gratitude*
> *And your words full of kindness*
> *May your heart be open, and joyously overflowing*
> *With compassion, forgiveness*
> *And love ....*

Live with Passion and Magnificence!
    Namaste.
        ~Z

(the beginning)

ABOUT THE AUTHOR

Z Newell lightly jokes that this book took sixty-two years to write. The stories shared here, including his bout with deadly Botulism, are powerful and touching. Z's background in psychology and philosophy—including sixteen years of men's personal transformation work—shine through.

Z is an inspirational speaker, author, consultant and trainer, and refers to himself as a *Transformation Catalyst*, because he helps to manifest the qualities that already exist within you. He is a Certified Life Coach, Certified Passion Test facilitator, and Certified ASAP Engagement Business Consultant.

Z currently lives in Lexington Kentucky, also known as the "Heart of the Bluegrass."

PREVIEW: Book two in this series, to be released in 2019, is titled *Ignite Your Magnificence AT WORK: How to GIVE YOUR ALL and LOVE IT*. It will address the relationship each of us has to our jobs or work, how to align our passion and purpose when facing resistance to our work and, ultimately, how to create personal Magnificence in that context.

Feel free to contact Z directly by email at z@znewellinspires.com with feedback on this book, or to hire him to speak to your company or organization. His primary speaker website is znewell.com.

[NOTE: Z's first book, a visionary novel titled *BRINK: Don't Go Back to Sleep* illustrates the slow unfolding of the MQformula process described in this book. A preview can be found at WhatMadeMeThink.com/Brink.]

www.ingramcontent.com/pod-product-compliance
Lightning Source LLC
Chambersburg PA
CBHW070603010526
44118CB00012B/1442